Cultural History and Postmodernity

M

Mark Poster

Cultural History and Postmodernity

DISCIPLINARY READINGS AND CHALLENGES

COLUMBIA UNIVERSITY PRESS • NEW YORK

Columbia University Press
Publishers Since 1893
New York   Chichester, West Sussex
Copyright © 1997 Columbia University Press
All rights reserved
Library of Congress Cataloging-in-Publication Data
Poster, Mark.
    Cultural history and postmodernity : disciplinary readings and
challenges / Mark Poster.
        p.   cm.
    Includes bibliographical references and index.
    ISBN 0–231–10882–6 (cloth : alk. paper). —
    ISBN 0–231–10883–4 (pbk. : alk. paper)
    1. Historiography.   2. History—Philosophy.
    3. Postmodernism.   4. Structuralism (Literary Analysis).
    I. Title.
    D13.P585   1997   96–48854
    907'.2—dc21   CIP

Casebound editions of Columbia University Press books are printed
on permanent and durable acid-free paper.
Printed in the United States of America
c 10 9 8 7 6 5 4 3 2 1
p 10 9 8 7 6 5 4 3 2 1

For Annette and the moment

Contents

Acknowledgments

I am deeply grateful for the comments offered by colleagues and friends. "Textual Agents" was read and critiqued by Jonathan Wiener and Joyce Appleby. "Furet" was read and commented on by the Critical Theory Institute at the University of California, Irvine; Linda Kaufman; Joan Landes; Leslie Rabine; Jacques Revel; John Rowe; Daniel Sherman; Timothy Tackett; and Torbjørn Wandel. "Lawrence Stone" was read by Nancy Armstrong, Joan Scott, Carroll Smith-Rosenberg, and the seminar on poststructuralism and history at the Humanities Research Institute of the University of California (held in summer 1990).

Part of the introduction appeared in a different version as "Poststructuralism and History: A Position," in *Gestos* 7, no. 14 (November 1992): 21–26. "Michel de Certeau and the History of Consumerism" appeared as "The Question of Agency: De Certeau and the History of Consumption," in *diacritics* 22, no. 2 (summer 1992): 94–107. "The Future According to Foucault" appeared as "The Future According to Foucault: Intellectual History and *The Archeology of Knowledge*," in Dominick La-Capra ed., *Modern European Intellectual History* (Ithaca: Cornell University Press, 1982), pp. 137–52.

Cultural History and Postmodernity

Introduction

Since the 1960s the discipline of history has grudgingly made room for the new genre of "social history." In the 1980s another new genre has emerged among historians, this one called "cultural history."[1] The profession's acceptance of social history followed a ragged course characterized by stages of denial, resistance, debate, approval, and, finally, hegemony. In the course of two decades social history changed from a scorned, marginal discourse referred to by leading political historians as "pots and pans history" into the prevailing norm of the field. The generation of young historians in the 1960s and 1970s who took some risks with their careers by practicing social history now to a considerable extent dominates the discipline. And this generation is currently defending its way of doing history against the new challengers, the cultural historians. In some cases, the senior generation of historians, such as Gertrude Himmelfarb, who predated the wave of social history and generally opposed it during the 1970s, now adamantly defend the current regime, including Marxist versions, against the new trend.[2]

The introduction of social history into the discipline brought with it a series of methodological innovations. Historians attended to the procedures of the social sciences: explanatory strategies shifted from narrative to analysis; evidence changed from the direct quotation of individuals to quantitative documentation; topics and problems concerned not political and intellectual elites but large groups and massive institutions of daily life; above all, the subjects of history were expanded from the political and intellectual elite to the working classes, women, the poor, criminals, and minority ethnic and racial groups. Taken together, these novelties constituted an epistemological break or paradigm shift of serious proportions. Yet I contend that aspects of the fundamental relation of the historian to the past were untouched by the upheaval. In particular, the shift from political to social history maintained a central feature of historiography: truth as the unmediated relation of the historian to the past.

The turn to social history also meant in particular a preference for "history from below," as its premier practitioner, E. P. Thompson, termed it.[3] This apparent change in direction, a focus on the bottom of the social order rather than a view from above, nonetheless retained a humanist view of the historical agent. Paraphrasing Marx for the discipline of history, Thompson wrote lines that few historians—liberal, conservative, or Marxist—would contest: "Men make their own history. They are part agent, part victim: it is precisely the element of agency which distinguishes them from the beasts, which is the *human* part of man."[4] Thompson thus spoke for a broad consensus of the discipline, even though social historians conceived their work as a radical departure from the ways of the older generation. Humanist to the bone, social and political historians alike defined history as the free and determined acts of agents. Masters and victims of their fates, these historical agents were the main characters in the drama of modern society, in both its capitalist and its socialist versions. The secret collusion of social and political historians rested in their fundamental unity on the question of the subject or agent, one that, to quote Thompson once more, "was present at its own making."[5] This fullness of presence of the individual or group to itself in its experience is the hallmark of the culture of modernity in the West. Any discourse that pretends to be critical of the prevailing order, call it "modern" or call it "capitalist," must begin by putting this figure of the self into question. This is what social and political historians have not been able to do, and this is the exact purpose of cultural history in its poststructuralist versions.

In both the "old" political-intellectual history and the "new" social history, the historian sought to attain the truth about the "real."[6] The records examined by the historian—diplomatic correspondence or local archives—were taken as transparent mediations between the past and the present. Textuality, writing, discourse, terms that poststructuralists have made into indications of a problematic, did not intercede between the historian and the representation of the past. Written traces were merely the occasion in which the gaze of the historian perceived directly the real that once was. The events and structures of the past drew all the attention of the old political historian and the new social historian. To read closely the documents as internally articulated signifiers, to take them seriously on their own structural terms, to consider self-reflexively their rhetorical shaping powers over the reader, to allow the text a material role in constituting historical knowledge: these are negligible digressions not suitable for the political or social historian impatient to recapture the "real." Like historical documents, the historian's discourse was itself another more or less elegantly composed transparent mediation. When Hayden White suggested otherwise in *Metahistory*[7]—that the trope embedded in the historical text greatly shaped its meaning—he was virtually ejected from the guild.

The new cultural history upsets this configuration of truth. It often does so by resorting to poststructuralist interpretive strategies and raising the issue of feminist and anticolonial discourse. The topic of women, for example, may provide the occasion for reexamining the relation of the historian to the truth because women have been figured in Western history as other to the truth, as outside the couplet truth-real. Writing the history of women, subjects who by and large have not authored the documents or at least those taken seriously by earlier generations of historians, as Joan Scott points out, calls attention to the text as noise, as interference between the historian and the truth, in addition to opening a new domain of the history of women.[8] Similarly, poststructuralist theory directly problematizes the text as mediation. In Derrida's case, the text is as much an indication of the absence of the real as it is itself an inscription of reality. For Foucault, as I will subsequently show, the textual document is material in the sense that discourse is productive of practice. Cultural history, then, challenges historians to confront what hitherto has remained buried in realist or logocentric assumptions of the representational power of writing, that is, the productive materiality of the text, the sense in which history as past event is always mediated by written documents and history as a form of knowledge is always itself a discourse.

There is another way of addressing the issue of epistemological self-consciousness and its relation to poststructuralist theory within the discipline of history. Historians often do not see the relevance of poststructuralist theory to their work because as a rule they do not seriously question what they do as a form of knowledge.[9] As long as historians fail to write texts that call into question the issue of knowledge and of their role in its production, poststructuralism will appear to them to be opaque, esoteric, and irrelevant. For in the first instance poststructuralism is a means of bringing into the open and putting into doubt the way a text organizes itself as a form of knowledge, as truth. Some poststructuralists, notably Derrideans, raise this issue for properly epistemological reasons. Others, like Foucault, with whom I am most in sympathy, raise the issue for political reasons as well.

The question of the truth claims of texts is particularly relevant at this time, it could be shown, because certain forms of discourse in the social sciences have become, in the contemporary university and the welfare state, inextricably merged with structures of domination. Therefore the failure to question the truth claims of the historian's writing or text operates by default to legitimize those forms of domination, to give cultural force to the hegemonic configuration of representationality. In other words, impatience with the issue of the truth status of one's text, the urge to get on with the seemingly more important business of analyzing change and attributing causes to events, is a form of representation that inadvertently plays into the hands of the established power structure and functions in a conservative way to authorize increasingly questionable and ubiquitous forms of representational discourse. Historical "explanations," for example, inscribe reason into the past in a manner that both controls it and introduces into it an instrumentality that mirrors that of the prevailing state and economic system. This effect of a certain form of representational discourse, I argue, applies even to those types of historical writing, such as historical materialism, that wish to be understood as critical or revolutionary.

In fairness, it might be noted that historical writing in turn raises questions for poststructuralism, especially in its deconstructionist variant. Historians are often masters of contextualization, practitioners of the art of tracing connections between different registers. Many deconstructionists, once outside the written text, seem uncertain and confused, overcome by what appears to them an infinite array of possible contextual relations, each with equally legitimate claim to the standing of "the context." This sense of confusion, or recognition of multiplicity, safeguards deconstruction from simplistic reductions. But it also may incapacitate it in the areas of history and politics by weakening its ability to present forceful, compelling interpretations of practices. Moreover, deconstruction may be responsible for its relative inability to treat the question of context: its very strength as a strategy of reading texts may produce a theoretical weakness when the object of analysis is not properly textual. Its insight is also blindness.

Weakening Oppositions and Blurred Distinctions

The field of cultural history as distinct from both intellectual history and social history may be configured in numerous ways. Roger Chartier, for instance, offers a starting point for a definition of cultural history as the calling into question of three traditional distinctions in intellectual and social history: high versus popular culture, production versus consumption, and reality versus fiction.[10] And surely these oppositions form an excellent starting point for thinking about a new cultural history as distinct from intellectual and social history. In relation to the first distinction, intellectual history drew its borders around the great works of thought, literature, and to a lesser extent the arts; popular culture, to the contrary, has been studied commonly by social historians using quantitative analysis or searching for indications of resistance against oppression. At times these clear lines between the subdisciplines of intellectual and social history were transgressed, as Robert Darnton did in the direction of a social history of intellectual life in his study of the diffusion of the Encyclopedia.[11] But these exceptions have been rare.

Chartier discusses the second distinction, that between production and consumption, in relation to intellectual and artistic creation versus reception. Before the recent interest in cultural history, creation was understood as the domain of intellectual history, and reception or reading was seen as part of social history. The production/consumption distinction goes to the heart of modern culture since it speaks to the profound value modernity places on the active, Faustian moment associated with the former term and the general disregard even antipathy in which the latter term, associated with passivity, is held. The rise of postmodern culture, with its fascination with consumerism and digital communications, with hypertext programs inverting readers into authors, dissolves the older priorities along with the binary opposition underlying them. At the theoretical level, Michel de Certeau in France and Cultural Studies in England demonstrated the "active" component of daily life among the popular classes. Walking in a city, reading a magazine, watching television, even participating in a fan club were reinterpreted as creative practices that resist hegemonic flows of imposition and constraint.[12]

Chartier's distinction between reality and fiction speaks to the stability of representational practices in the modern period, the sense that texts firmly point outside themselves to referents that are understood as distinct. This opposition relies on the Cartesian dualism of bodies and minds in which individuals are subjects metaphysically distinct from objects. Intellectual history treats subjects and their spiritual creations, literary and philosophical representations of external worlds. Social history inevitably configures its field as one of objects, material things determined by laws, forces, and tendencies (even though the agent of the social historian is surely a Cartesian subject). Cultural history emerges as a possibility when this distinction begins to collapse, when the performative aspects of language are recognized. In Chartier's words, "What is real, in fact, is not (or not only) the reality that the text aims at, but the very manner in which it aims at it in the historic setting of its production and the strategy used in its writing."[13] Texts do more and less than represent: they configure what they point to, and they are configured by it. To the extent that discourse configures what it indicates, it is a fiction as much as a representation. When reality and fiction are seen as permeable to one another, material reality has a cultural component, and culture is material.

While these distinctions do not sharply delineate all that is at stake in the new field of cultural history, they are helpful in outlining a changed context for debate. They suggest directions for study; they hint at new perspectives and new topics; they validate imaginative proposals and open the gates to heterodox formulations, tearing down the defenses of disciplinary stability. One might now comb the archives for documents on advertising or cosmetics or comic books, topics earlier regarded as of grand vulgarity, of stupendous banality, and still discover through their investigation the key to working-class politics or women's identity or a youth culture imaginary. What is perhaps worse from the standpoint of the stable dichotomy of intellectual and social history, one might also mix the levels, the types of discourses, the realms of high and low. Thus cultural history may study the influence of the legal system on the development of psychoanalysis,[14] or the relation of a play by Shakespeare to colonial life in Virginia,[15] or the connection between modernist art and psychology and of both with advertising.[16] A vertiginous array of possibilities confronts the would-be cultural historian.

Cultural History and Subject Constitution

Cultural history's fluid multiplication of research agendas is salubrious for the discipline of history. Productive affinities link cultural history to emerging perspectives such as discourse analysis, deconstruction, new historicism, and cultural studies. Connective tissues bind the subdiscipline to theoretico-political clusters such as postcolonialism, subaltern studies, queer theory, and feminist studies. Amid the proliferating proposals and initiatives, one problematic stands out in my mind as a most promising line of study in cultural history: that is, the question of the construction of the subject. Cultural history might then be understood as the study of the construction of the subject, the extent to which and the mechanisms through which individuals are attached to identities, the shapes and characteristics of those identities, the role the process of self-constitution plays in the disruption or stabilization of political formations, and the relation of all these processes to distinctions of gender, ethnicity, and class.

The issues at stake in this cultural history are profound. For as long as historians presuppose that their task is to discover or investigate agents and victims, to resurrect for the present age fully formed agents in the past bearing and resisting burdens of oppression, there can never be a historiography that is critical of modernity simply because a world of agents and victims is its chief cultural figure, its great ideological myth. Historians may contribute to the delineation of the limits of the modern only by studying how such a cultural figure (the individual or group as agent/victim) was constituted. This task, I propose, is the preem-

inent one for cultural history: to trace the construction of the autonomous agent, with due attention to its differential predecessors, and to estimate the extent to which it may be at a point of
decline, in other words, the extent to which a postmodern cultural figure, one yet to be clearly defined, may be emerging. Such
a project of cultural history benefits from the critique of Western
culture at the heart of poststructuralist theory, especially in the
Foucaultian and Derridean forms. It also finds natural allies in
those discursive orientations that derive from a position of exteriority with respect to the cultural dominant of the modern West,
that is, postcolonialism, subaltern theory, feminist theory, and
queer theory. And this cultural history would benefit from certain advances already at play in disciplines from literature to sociology such as new historicism and cultural studies. Finally, one
must understand my proposal for a cultural history not as sup-
planting or displacing social and political history but as challenging them, as animating the discipline by the introduction of a
different way of doing history, a different set epistemological
protocols.

The question I raise under the banner of cultural history for
my colleagues who have critical ambitions is then the following:
if modern society claims to promote the freedom of the individual, how can one define its limits except by showing that "free
individuals" are historical constructions? Otherwise the historian projects a figure of the free individual into the past, duly
noting and regretting the unjust impositions upon it yet confirming the great myth of modernity. The truly historical task is
not to find in the past suffering workers and victimized women
so that all may recognize the evils of the system. Instead the
problem is to describe the mechanisms through which such people were constituted as subjects in relation to the measure of
stable, centered autonomy; to show how the discursive figure
of the universal, free individual was paradoxically able to desig-
nate these groups and others as outside the universal and as
unfree, to show that modern freedom has always only been possible through its exclusions. This task will reveal that the mod-

ern nation has always been a forced and false unity, a seductive goal whose only realization must be its systematic undoing. Cultural historians contribute to a critical history when they show not that certain groups were wrongly excluded from the nation but that the proper goal of emancipation is for all to strive for such exclusion.

In addition to the question of a cultural history of the constitution of the subject, I bring to this work a perception of the importance of a particular determination of the contemporary context: the increasing role of electronically mediated communication. As will be clear in what follows, I take seriously the emergence of a postmodern culture through the dissemination of technologies that reconfigure space and time, the relation of human to machine and mind to body. These technologies, not in themselves but as they are installed in space through specific practices, are drastically altering the conditions under which the subject is constituted, indeed even the subject who writes history. Just as the emergence of the capitalist mode of production promoted stances through which the entire past could be rethought and its history rewritten, so the emergence of electronic and now digital modes of information opens new positions and instantiates new viewpoints about the past. The challenge for the discipline of history is not simply to assimilate poststructuralist and other new intellectual trends to its particular needs and uses, not simply to carve out a new domain of cultural history with new topics and new modes of self-reflexive writing, but to do these with an eye to a new context of globalizing and virtualizing communication practices, practices that, it must be kept in mind, alter the intellectual trends and the domain of culture.

The Aim of the Book; or, How I Would Like to Be Read

My method of procedure in what follows is to examine carefully one historical work or closely related group of works in each chapter, looking for characteristic disciplinary gestures or rules of formation that close the text(s) from a historical perspective on the modern individual or agent. I do this generally by reading the texts through poststructuralist lenses. My purpose is not to ridicule, condemn, or even criticize the authors of these works but to detect the characteristic principles of the contemporary discipline and test their limits as vehicles of critique. I have selected works by historians I particularly admire or hold in great esteem generally because they themselves have pushed the limits of the discipline in one respect or another. I have tried as much as possible to avoid a polemical tone or to elicit heated, defensive responses. My aim is to enliven the discipline, to open it to intellectual currents that seem productive of new critical strategies. Yet I know that what I am offering is controversial and that the positions I regard as glorious insights will be regarded by some as heresies, or foolishness, or worse. As Nietzsche writes and Foucault writes again, discourses emerge in a field of relations of power, defying some, supporting others, hardly coming into the scholarly world as innocent pursuits of truth. I hope that my colleagues will appreciate this condition of disciplinary argument and engage themselves in the strife of divergent rationalities.

1

Lawrence Stone's Family History

> History has always had many mansions, and must continue to do so if it is to flourish in the future. The triumph of any one *genre* or school eventually always leads to narrow sectarianism, narcissism and self-adulation, contempt or tyranny towards outsiders, and other disagreeable and self-defeating characteristics.
>
> —*Lawrence Stone, "The Revival of Narrative"*

In this chapter I shall focus on two specific sorts of questions poststructuralist theory raises for the discipline of history: one concerning its epistemological and methodological assumptions regarding the historian's strategy of reading; the other concerning its object, organizing theme, conceptual apparatus, and repertoire of topics.

The Way Historians Read Themselves

Poststructuralists think that reading texts is central to disciplines in the humanities and, in particular, find much to fault with the way historians read documents of the past. Most historians think of reading texts as a subordinate, even peripheral, part of their work, certainly not a central aspect of it. They define their field as the analysis and explanation of change in the world and strongly resent redefinitions of the field by literary people talking of textual interpretation. Historians are pleased by works of history that are rich in detail, coherent in narrative, and convincing in explanatory power. By and large they do not recognize themselves in the attacks on history presented by poststructuralists; they do not see much connection between the problems of reading and interpretation raised by poststructuralists and the day-to-day labors of Clio.

This disparity of perspectives troubles me since I am both a historian and someone who finds much of the writings of poststructuralists to be of vital importance to what I do. I shall show that historical writing can be enhanced by studying poststructuralist theory and that historical writing that defines itself as critical especially benefits by this study. I will first briefly explicate some relevant aspects of Michel Foucault's writing on history and then discuss the work of one historian, Lawrence Stone, to show how a lack of sensitivity to issues raised by poststructuralists leads to problems in Stone's text. Lawrence Stone provides a good case in point because his work is highly regarded by historians and because he is notorious for his lack of interest in poststructuralism. He has been known to say, for example, that there is no reason for historians to read Foucault.

Foucault and the Subject in History

Foucault complains that mainstream historical writing is flawed because, among other things, it reinforces the notion that the individual is a coherent entity, unified by a power of rational thought. Historians would in great majority, I suppose, deny this accusation with the retort that this statement is needlessly abstract and theoretical. If they find such individuals in history they will report it; if not, they will not regret their absence. For historians, this concern represents a typical case of a poststructuralist misunderstanding of the historical project. The historian might go further and argue that human beings are complex, often inscrutable, creatures, far from the unified or centered beings who bother Foucault.

Foucault's point nonetheless is that historians make the assumption of a pregiven or centered subject and present the past as a continuous development that draws together and merges into one the dead and the living, the subjects of history and the historian. He puts it this way:

> Continuous history is the indispensable correlative of the founding function of the subject: the guarantee that everything that has eluded him may be restored to him; the certainty that time will disperse nothing without restoring it in a reconstituted unity; the promise that one day the subject—in the form of historical consciousness—will once again be able to appropriate, to bring back under his sway, all those things that are kept at a distance by difference, and find in them what might be called his abode.[1]

Instead of writing history as if the subject were already formed as a rational individual inhibited from realizing this state only by irrational institutions, Foucault proposes that history concern itself with the way individuals become subjects, the mechanisms through which individuals are defined as autonomous from the world of objects and fundamentally rational, as having a "truth." Foucault's historical project takes as its problem the process of subjectivization, the complex of discourses and practices through which subjects are constituted. Such a project, he thinks, allows the historian to make a historical question out of what is often taken for granted: that in history individuals have self-interest, which they pursue rationally. As much as Foucault insists on it, historians deny that they commit the intellectual mistake of taking for granted precisely what needs to be questioned. I shall show that Lawrence Stone commits the error of assuming the historical reality of the subject and that this materially reduces the power of his text.

Stone in History

Lawrence Stone established his position as an early leading practitioner of social history with pathbreaking books on the English gentry—*Crisis of the Aristocracy* (1965) and *Family and Fortune: Studies in Aristocratic Finance in the Sixteenth and Seventeenth Centuries* (1973)—and on the family—*The Family, Sex and Marriage in England, 1500–1800* (1977); *Road to Divorce: England, 1530–1987* (1990); *Uncertain Unions: Marriage in England, 1660–1753* (1992); and *Broken Lives: Separation and Divorce in England, 1660–1857* (1993). From 1969 to the late 1980s he directed the Shelby Cullom Davis Center at Princeton University, which, during his tenure, devoted yearly seminars to topics in social history, including the family, education, youth, and the like. Aspiring social historians from around the country have presented their ideas at the center, benefiting from the lively comments of the participants. Independent of any history department, the Davis Center under Stone's tutelage has been a unique disciplinary institution, promoting the cause of social history and providing an unusual arena for the discussion of empirical and methodological issues. In these respects, as both an institution builder and an active scholar, Lawrence Stone has been a leader in the field of social history.

In 1977 Stone published *The Family, Sex and Marriage in England, 1500–1800*, a book that has been widely recognized as a classic of family history, one that is praised for its scholarship, writing, and analytic powers, although it has been a subject of controversy for feminist historians and others.[2] Despite the fact that in recent years Stone has published several books on the related topic of divorce,[3] for purposes of economy and concentration I shall limit my analysis to his study of the family. *The Family, Sex and Marriage* presents a broad overview of the English family since the Renaissance, with particular emphasis on the emergence of the modern nuclear family. Until its appearance, the standard work on the English family was Peter Laslett's

The World We Have Lost, which favored a demographic view of
family history in which continuity of family size predominates.
Laslett argued that the nuclear family of modernity actually
dates from the sixteenth century, if not earlier. He writes that
"household size was remarkably constant in England at 4.75 persons per household at all times from the late sixteenth century
until the early twentieth century."[4] Laslett's quantitative analysis
of parish registers debunked the conventional sociological wisdom of a large extended family in preindustrial, rural society being replaced, as a consequence of the industrial revolution, by a
small, private nuclear family. Now widely accepted by historians, the demographer's picture of a long nuclear family, if I may
use that phrase, seriously eviscerated the conception of a dense
fabric of domestic sociability in favor of a numerical accounting
of blood relations residing under the same roof. This view ignored workers, apprentices, even animals, who participated in
the daily life of the household. It elided the life cycles of families,
at some points of which three generations all resided together. It
ignored the fact that children, the center of the nuclear family,
did *not* reside with the family through their crucial formative
years but were shipped off as apprentices and lived with
strangers. Worst of all, Laslett placed little importance on the
emotional patterns, symbolic structures, and relational hierarchies that distinguish in sharp discontinuity the early modern
from the modern family. Lawrence Stone's considerable accomplishment was to correct for the demographic reductionism of
The World We Have Lost by addressing the issue of the family's
role in the creation of the self.

As a genre of historical writing, *The Family, Sex and Marriage
in England* is a "formation," or "origins," or "rise" book, a common form among historians of both politics and society. The centuries it treats, the sixteenth, seventeenth, and eighteenth, are
called the "early modern period." This designation suggests a
continuity with the subsequent centuries, serving to unify the
past five hundred years under the term *modern*. As a "rise" book,

The Family, Sex and Marriage begins with a depiction of a pre-modern family type and traces its change into a properly modern form. Stone's period is then divided into three overlapping stages, each having its own family type: (1) "the open lineage family," from 1450 to 1630; (2) "the restricted patriarchal nuclear family," from 1550 to 1700; and (3) "the closed domesticated nuclear family," from 1640 to 1800. Stone devotes 40 pages to phase one; 100 pages to phase two; and 330 pages to phase three. A conclusion briefly treats "post-1800" developments: 14 pages on the nineteenth century and 2 on the twentieth century. By its structure and emphasis, then, Stone's text focuses on the emergence of the nuclear family in the eighteenth century.

Stone's problem in the book is to "explain" this "rise." He devotes a separate section to the question of explanation or interpretation, as he calls it, thereby attempting to keep interpretation apart from the main, descriptive-analytic body of the work. "Interpretations of the Change, 1640–1800" begins with an assertion of what is changing: "What needs explaining is not a change of structure, or of economics, or of social organization, but of sentiment."[5] This is an argument against Marxist economic determination, and Stone is insistent that the rise of the nuclear family is not a consequence of the industrial revolution, as both Friedrich Engels and followers of Talcott Parsons thought. Of course, by centering his interpretation on a shift of "sentiment," he extracts the problem from the domain of economics altogether.

The nuclear family for Stone promotes a certain configuration of sentiment that he labels "affective individualism." Unlike "the open lineage family" or the "restricted patriarchal nuclear family" of the earlier period, "the closed domesticated nuclear family," or modern family, raises children to be affective individuals. Stone borrows the idea of affective individualism from a nexus of vaguely Freudian positions most clearly developed by the neo-Parsonian writing of Platt and Weinstein, in which the autonomous, free individual is the product of the nuclear family.[6] This individualism was nurtured in the child-care practices of emerging nuclear families, along with a new burgeoning of warm feelings between parents and children.[7] Although the question of individualism is surely one of the deepest and most difficult in Western culture, Stone's discussion of it, as often is the case when historians treat theoretical issues, is loose and imprecise. All too briefly he characterizes the term *individualism* as a combination of "introspection" and "a demand for personal autonomy" (p. 223). He provides no hint of the ideological implications of these politically charged traits, the way they may function to occlude the individual's imbrication with social relations, as Western Marxists would claim, or the way individualism may exalt certain ethnic, racial, and gender groupings over others. Nor does he recognize how the values of introspection and personal autonomy may be the cultural effect of a certain way of constituting the subject, as Foucault would argue, rather than being simple, positive characteristics. Thus, while Stone's book goes beyond demographics to address the major cultural issue of the construction of the modern subject, his execution of this shift is fraught with difficulties.

As an empirical social historian, Stone is uncomfortable with theory, which for him is separate from and incompatible with facts. Grudgingly he writes that "the rise of Affective Individualism seems best to fit the confused and conflicting evidence" (p. 687). Through the maze of historical specificities, through the countless "unique events" that Stone simply finds, perceives, discovers always already somehow "in" the documents—and accomplishing this without the slightest need for "theory"—the historian, the modest grubber among the archives, still finds it within himself, finds himself authorized to make what must be considered rather grandiose judgments. For example, the rise of Affective Individualism is, in Stone's words, "one of the most significant transformations that has ever taken place," and this "not only in the most intimate aspects of human life"—the topic Stone has actually researched—"but also in the nature of social organization" (p. 687), a large topic about which Stone has presented no indication of systematic research or thinking. Here we have it then: Stone's book is an account of (one of the) most important affairs of all human life.

Stone's unselfconscious and self-designated authority, his ease with broad assertion, while perhaps on the wane among historians nowadays, is characteristic of the way the discipline of history grounds itself, the way it produces foundationalist statements. Stone's assertion of the importance of his finding is the payoff of the book, the anchor that stabilizes the text, that organizes, with great centripetal force, six hundred and fifty pages of unique events into a single meaning. The easy confidence of the historian on display in the above quotation from Stone has a musty, out-of-date ring to it, bespeaking a time when the discipline of history was staffed by men from the social elite, men who habitually made these sorts of judgments about what is important in the world and what is not, passing their values on to a small audience of upper-class students who were in training for political and economic leadership. The command and assurance in Stone's statement perhaps distinguishes him from the current generation of social historians who rose in the profession during the massive expansion of higher education in the 1960s and 1970s and are wary of grand pronouncements about "the most significant transformation that has ever taken place." Yet the discomfort of many historians today with such judgments denotes a crisis of confidence as much as a rejection of Stone's interpretive maneuver. Historians no longer feel comfortable presenting a grand narrative of Western, much less human, development in which the task of distinguishing what is most important from what is less important flows easily.

Stone is somewhat more careful in characterizing the overall trajectory of the history of the family than in informing his readers about the significance of the family in human affairs. He denies outright that the history of the family is one of continuous and linear evolution: "It is wholly false to assume that there can have been any such thing as straightforward linear development [of the nuclear family]." Nor does he want to give the impression of the nuclear family's eternity: "There is no reason to assume that the end-product of affective individualism . . . is any more permanent an institution than were the many family types which preceded it" (pp. 682–83). Stone explains the variations, bumps, twists, and turns in the development of the nuclear family by resorting to a liberal pluralist "eternal conflict of interests and values" that he thinks is somehow different from "linear development." Immediately after this statement he writes that "this is strongly suggested by the fact that the cause of change lies in an unending dialectic of competing interests and ideas" (p. 683). His confusions in this crucial "causal" statement are pronounced: (1) he presents the "cause of change" as that which it precisely is not, that is to say, a "fact," (2) he presents a "dialectic of competing interests and ideas" as "unending," whereas dialectics are actually full of resolutions and syntheses or ends, and (3) he surreptitiously elevates "interests and ideas" to the status of prime movers without the slightest effort at discursive justification. Stone also directly contradicts the explicit intention of the text: he introduces "straightforward linear evolution" in the liberal pluralist form of his "dialectic of eternal conflict of interests and values" while denying that he is doing so. Such a display of incoherence hides important theoretical issues from the historian's ken.

The Historian's Reasons

The Family, Sex, and Marriage suffers from a problem of continuity, as addressed in the quotation from Foucault cited earlier in the chapter. The book constitutes the historian as the centered, rational subject of history. I will present several passages from the body of Stone's text to prove this point. The first concerns the relation, during the early modern period, between poor parents and their children on the issue of marriage. On this subject Stone writes, "the family and kin interest in the marriage of the propertyless was low *since* no money or land changed hands, and the incentive to interfere was *consequently* limited. Marriage among the poor, we *must assume*, was far more a personal than a family and kin affair" (p. 92; emphasis added). Stone is here contrasting marriage among the wealthier classes, in which, as he had already shown, parents chose marriage partners for their children, with that among the poor. In the case of the latter group, he does not present evidence but instead makes an assumption and offers a conclusion. In this case, we can say that he is reading past the textual documents, but on what basis is he doing so?

Stone "must assume" that marriage choice among the poor was not an important concern of parents *because* there was no exchange of property. He further "must assume" that exchange of property is the reason for parental interference in the marriage choices of their children. In attempting to interpret Stone's reading, I will first reject the hypothesis that he is a crude historical materialist, applying a theoretical principle by which all social acts are determined by the mode of production, so that the passing-on of property shapes family affairs. Instead Stone is doing something less and something more than this. If we return to Foucault's argument about "continuity" and the centered subject, we can say that Stone is filling in a gap in the historical texts (they do not say why poor parents left marriage choices to their children, or even if they did grant their children this right). By filling in this gap in the way that he does, he erases the *difference* between poor early modern parents and himself. He is reading their acts in the way that makes sense of them for himself, that provides a kind of coherence to the past that gives him a feeling of unity with it. Although distant from the early modern poor in every way, he nonetheless finds/projects a meaning in the past that serves to assure him that motivations he deems rational in the present are confirmed by the past.

This fabricated coherence also confers mastery or control over the past. The knowledge Stone produces in his text is a form of domination over the past, one that domesticates potential disruptive features of the past, such as threatening differences represented by the poor, women, and non-nuclear families. To the extent that the family of Affective Individualism becomes the telos of Stone's narrative, it is naturalized and legitimated. The nuclear family, heterosexuality, romantic love, and individualism are empowered in his discourse by its knowledge effect. This is a political aspect of historical writing that often goes unrecognized or is positively disavowed. To the extent that Stone writes a narrative without gaps between himself and his subject, one that covers both the entire period and all the various groups within it, he has produced an ostensibly full knowledge, a complete account, a satisfying discourse, a putatively true representation that makes claims as knowledge but also intervenes as power. The topic of marriage choices among poor families, along with Stone's reasons and explanations for such behavior, then, is not a marginal issue but one that affects the epistemological status of his overall project. Precisely at the margins of his text—the poor and their lack of documentation—Stone resorts to interpretative strategies that determine the truth of his discourse at its center concerning the upper and middle classes about whom evidence is more plentiful. Everywhere the historian casts his gaze property motivates parents to intervene in the choice of mates for their children.

Stone notwithstanding, poor parents of the period might well have chosen mates for their children, although so few traces of their decisions remain extant that generalizations are hazardous. Stone excludes this possibility only because the poor lacked the property he deemed the sole reason for parents interfering in their children's choices of mate. But other reasons to interfere are quite legitimately possible to consider. One social group higher in status than the early modern poor as Stone defines them, the peasants, in many cases regulated their lives by village traditions, by moral rules, and one of these was the principle of hierarchy, more specifically patriarchal authority, although this factor, we are now learning, may have been overemphasized in the past as a characteristic of early modern Europe. Fathers might well have chosen mates for their children simply because they were fathers, older men who were higher in the social hierarchy than their children were. In other words, it is likely that fathers made the choice merely because that is what fathers did:, make all important decisions about individuals who were under their control, including their children. But this moral principle, hierarchy, does not hold much sway for the present-day historian.[8] It is an element of discontinuity between fathers in seventeenth-century England and fathers in late-twentieth-century America. So Stone erases the difference and imposes a unity between the past and the present by inventing a reason that makes sense to him— that property justifies parental interference—and assures the centeredness of his own subjectivity, an act of interpretation that poststructuralists would disallow.[9] If the mechanisms of strong patriarchal dominance were the starting point of an examination of poor families, the danger of invoking the rational subject as a link between the historian and the past might be avoided, precisely because such paternal dominance strikes the historian today as objectionable, distasteful and different from his or her own proclivities. An example of such a study is Foucault's *Discipline and Punishment*. In it, he sets forth a theory of "technologies of power" to investigate the torture system of punishment during early modern society, a system that is in sharp discontinuity with the carceral system of modernity and, by its very difference and repugnance to modern taste, can have the interpretive effect, he thinks, of delegitimizing and denaturalizing the claims of the modern institution.[10]

A second passage, this time concerning the emotional relation between parents and children, better illustrates the historian's problem of reading. Stone cites evidence that parents of the period in question did not love their children. To give the reader an example of the kind of evidence we have about parental feelings toward their children, let me cite one seventeenth-century French aristocratic mother's observation that "one blushes to think of loving one's children."[11] While this statement might be interpreted in many ways—for example, as a defensive rejoinder to a claim that children should be loved by their mothers—the minimal role of these noble mothers in child care and the low value they placed on it suggest a group sentiment very much different from today's. Here certainly is a bit of discontinuity, an attitude that today seems morally repugnant if not barbaric. What is the historian to make of this evidence? How is he or she to read the text of parental indifference to their children? Stone attempts to resolve the tension, to wipe out the difference, not by denying that it was so (although some historians do just that) but by providing an explanation for it, actually an alibi absolving parents of culpability for their different feelings even though they themselves might not wish to acknowledge any wrongdoing. Here is the way Stone puts it: "Between upper-class parents and children, relations in the sixteenth century were also usually fairly remote. One reason for this was the very high infant and child mortality rates, which made it folly to invest too much emotional capital in such ephemeral beings" (p. 105).

Infant mortality was by today's standards very high in the early modern period. Approximately half of the live births never survived to age twenty. Most parents therefore experienced the death of their own children, probably more than once. By contrast, modern parents rarely suffer this fate, and when they do they are likely to empathize with the mournful sounds of Gustav Mahler's song cycle, *Die Kindertotenlieder*, in which a child's death evokes immeasurable sadness. How shocking then for the historian to discover, even among the leading circles of early modern society, parents' callous impassivity toward their children. Of course, if these parents demonstrated little of what we call love, we must be careful not to exclude the possibility that the word meant something different to them than it does to us and that they may well have experienced constellations of feeling that are incommensurate with or have no parallel to what we feel toward our children.

But Stone accepts, I think correctly, the tendency, during this period, toward emotional distance between parents and children. The problem begins with his explanation for it: "one *reason* for this" was that it was "folly to invest too much emotional capital in such ephemeral beings." The problems here are numerous. First, there is the issue of a certain psychological theory being presented but not explicitly acknowledged. Stone implies that individuals have instrumental control over their feelings, that they "invest" feelings as they would capital, to achieve the greatest return. This is a utilitarian model of psychology that has little credibility. Second, the utilitarian model, whatever its current status as a psychological theory, is peculiarly anachronistic when inserted in the premodern context of aristocratic family life and employed as an explanation of behavior. Such models did not even arise until the late eighteenth century and may have had little currency in societies that were to some extent precapitalist. Instrumental rational action or utilitarian ethics, as Weber tells us, is characteristic of modern societies where markets and bureaucracies predominate. Thus Stone, by attributing modern motivations to premodern situations, thereby mitigates the force of the difference between the two. Third, the specific explanation he offers—that it is folly or unreasonable to love beings who might die and thereby cause grief—is decidedly gratuitous.

In both examples, the historian emerges as a crude reader of texts, an interpreter who is somewhat cavalier in inferring causes, extrapolating explanations, attributing reasons for things that bear little connection with the traces on the documents of the past. One might conclude from the example of *The Family, Sex and Marriage* that the task of historians indeed is not to read texts but to explain change and to do so almost absent-mindedly, without careful attention to the written corpus. One finds in Stone's text over and over again the use of the term *reason*, in the sense of "explanation," in just those places where the author has no evidence and is supplying thoughts of his own invention. *Explanation* in Stone's text is equivalent to fiction, but because it is unrecognized as such he cannot explore his need for this rhetorical move. Here is a third example, taken from the practice of hiring wet nurses: "One of the *reasons* for this system of sending new-born infants out to mercenary wet-nurses for the first year or more was that it made the appalling level of infant mortality much easier to bear" (p. 107; emphasis added). Again Stone cites no evidence that this was the case, neither that using wet nurses made infant mortality easier to bear nor that such was the "reason" for doing it. In fact, the opposite may have been the case in many instances: some wet nurses were known to the community as "killing nurses," and mothers who wished to dispose of unwanted or inconvenient offspring would choose these women.

The term *reason* in Stone's text functions as a bridge, a point of continuity between the historian and the past. It serves to link the mind of the author, his reason, with the past. The author puts or projects reasons into the past and, after finding the past a not unfriendly place, is reassured as to his own reasons in the present. Stone uses the term *reason* in precisely those places where the past was different and strange: parents sending out newborn babies or lacking affection for their children. Instead of holding on to the difference, seeing it as a way to undercut the sense of naturalness and legitimacy that surrounds present-day customs regarding these matters—which is Foucault's interpretive strategy—Stone chooses to erase the difference. The impression he gives is that of a generous, humane, wise scholar, one who uncovers the harsh living conditions of our ancestors and yet understands that their lives made sense in the face of hardship, that they too were human beings and responded much as we would under the circumstances. If parents didn't love their children, they had reasons for it, reasons that are not in the documents but in the mind of the twentieth-century humanist historian.

This is the way it goes with historical explanations. Historians explain changes and by so doing erase the difference between the past and the present. By erasing this difference, the rational subject is discursively installed in both the past and the present. What is called historical explanation is a discourse with political effects: the discourse discovers "truth" as explanation, and this explanation affirms the rationality of the historian, of the discipline of history. History, then, is a discursive strategy that has as one of its effects the installation and support of a centered subject and its political positions, be they liberal or Marxist. Historical explanation domesticates the past to the present, to the rational subject in the present (the historian) and to the political views of that subject. Foucault's genealogy, on the contrary, stresses the difference of the past, thereby unsettling the naturalness of the present. With regard to the question of the subject, Foucault raises the problem of how it was constructed, opening the process of construction to historical investigation. Stone closes the question of the subject by projecting it into the past and drawing a direct line of continuity between the past and the present.

The objection may be raised that my criticism of Stone's book, while perhaps valid, does not require any poststructuralist theory or, indeed, any theory at all, because Stone's errors are accounted for by the standard vigilance of the historian. Stone has simply spoken without having adequate evidence to support his case. While it is true that the evidentiary basis of Stone's statements about poor families is very slender, pointing out that failure is not the aim of my critique. I am concerned with historians' statements of explanation, and these may be found in other texts that are supported by mountains of evidence. In such cases, as in Stone's account of the early modern family, the so-called explanation has the following discursive form: reasons or causes are provided, and these reasons erase differences between the present and the past, linking the two in a chain of continuity.

In a later debate with Gertrude Himmelfarb over the merits of social history Stone reveals the strong political force behind the issue of reason in history. In a retort to Himmelfarb's attack on social history and other contemporary historiographical trends, Stone construes social history as the discipline of history's strongest bulwark of defense against threatening irrationalists: "Today we need to stand shoulder to shoulder against the growing army of enemies of rationality. By that I mean the followers of the fashionable cult of absolute relativism, emerging from philosophy, linguistics, semiotics, and deconstructionism. These are truly 'denigrating the power of reason,' since they tend to deny the possibility of accurate communication by the use of language, the force of logical deduction, and the very existence of truth and falsehood."[12] On the contrary, I contend that poststructuralist theory empowers the historian's critical understanding of the way the allegedly rational subject is historically constituted. Far from denying "the possibility of accurate communication" a Foucaultian study of the family might enable the historian to raise the issue of rationality in a critical, not derogatory, fashion. Instead of being an issue that interferes with the historian's grasp of nonmodern culture, reason becomes an aspect of the constitution of modern subjectivity.

And this is precisely what Jacques Donzelot, proceeding from Foucaultian theoretical directions, achieves in *The Policing of Families* for the history of the French family in the nineteenth and twentieth centuries. He shows how the modern family was not simply a nuclear family but actually divided into bourgeois and working-class forms. In each case, the family is enmeshed in complexes of institutions, practices, and discourses that belie its privacy and autonomy. Working-class families are regulated by the welfare state in the twentieth century and by a variety of voluntary organizations and charities in the nineteenth. Bourgeois families are normalized by medical and psychological groupings: "From being a locus of resistance to medical norms that threatened its integrity and the interplay of its privileges, the bourgeois family became the best surface of reception of these norms. . . . Birth control, psycho-pedagogy, and the preoccupation with relational life were added to a store that was already stocked with the bourgeois 'quality of life.' "[13] Instead of a telos of affective individualism, Donzelot opens family history to a complex analysis of discourses and practices that construct subject positions of very different types.

The History of What

It is a safe generalization to assert that historians write about topics that concern them and their audience in the present, even though some of their topics may arise from issues that are internal to the development of the discipline itself. With enough space one could show a correlation between current political issues and the topics chosen by historians. This is certainly true of family history, a subdiscipline that arose in the 1960s at a time when divorce rates rose sharply, abortion became widespread, gay liberation and feminism emerged as political movements—in short, when so many of the hallmarks of the nuclear family were questioned, even challenged in society at large. Until the 1960s, however, it is fair to say that two specific topics—politics and labor—engaged the attention of historians and that these topics are associated with the grand theories or metanarratives of liberalism and Marxism, whether or not historians explicitly acknowledged this relation. Historians wrote about the rise of the modern state—in particular, the institution of representative democracy—and about the industrial revolution—in particular, the institution of capitalism. The importance of these topics was taken for granted, just as the *un*importance of the histories of women, children, ethnic minorities, the family, and so many other topics currently fashionable among or at least acceptable to historians was also taken for granted.

Poststructuralism, I contend, also has something to say to historians about their choice of topics. Poststructuralist writing proceeds from the assumption that the metanarratives that gave urgency to the history of democracy and capitalism no longer hold their verisimilitude, no longer seem to make sense of the world to the same degree as perhaps they once did. This is an intuitive judgment, having no more truth value than that. The conviction among poststructuralists is that we are no longer able to make sense of our world by resorting to liberal and Marxist theories, that things have changed and the social formation no longer is rendered plausible or intelligible by resorting to the old positions. In particular, the feature of the old positions that stands in the way of their heuristic value is their strong assumption that the world is about action rather than language. Struggling against tyranny, fighting wars to preserve or expand the nation, building democratic or administrative institutions, organizing unions, inventing and innovating, working on the assembly line or the plantation: these are the real events of history. Hence the quizzical looks exchanged among many historians when a stray intellectual historian defines historical methodology as a strategy of reading texts.

Poststructuralist theories, on the other hand, are designed for the analysis of language; they begin to lose their capacity to display the world as intelligible to the degree that issues of action are at stake. This is a source of both their limitations and their strengths. My hypothesis is that the poststructuralist emphasis on language over action is concurrent with, though not reducible to, a similar change of priorities in the social sphere of the technologically developed societies. In the military, deeds of valor in battle have been replaced by scientific-technical discourses; in the capitalist economy, the problem of increasing production by organizing labor and subduing the forces of nature has been replaced by the need to increase consumption through the language of advertising. Social control through generalized misery combined with carceral institutions has given way to ubiquitous monitoring and disciplinary credentialing. In politics, the shift from Boss Tweed to Ronald Reagan represents a change from taking care of one's own to appearing to be like oneself, from acts of patronage to simulational images of friendliness.

Poststructuralist theories have their dangers: they do not recognize parallels between philosophical turns to language and social changes, and they do not favor the contextualizing of interpretive strategies, especially of their own positions. Some deconstructionists, for example, begin and end with texts and yet claim somehow to have always already accounted for history-society-politics (all of which often appear in their writing as an undifferentiated list) *in the margins* of texts. Many historians have been suspicious of poststructuralist positions, which appear to them to be reincarnations of the formalist anti-Marxism and substantive conservatism of New Criticism. On the rare occasion when deconstructionists venture beyond the boundaries of the text, such historians complain, the results are often disappointing, if not genuinely disturbing. Historians are easily frustrated by poststructuralist discussions of nuclear war that treat this potential holocaust as epistolary novel,[14] by discussions of apartheid that contain no reference to imperialism,[15] or by books on history by poststructuralist writers who rarely engage the historian's problematic.[16] These historians may resort to Dr. Johnson's tactic of kicking the rock and asking if the toe hurts. "The truck that is coming down the road," warns historian Allen Megill, "is fundamentally different from the interpretation 'Here comes a truck.' "[17] And, one might add, a writer like Paul de Man, who published one hundred essays in a fascist periodical, many of which extolled fascist writers and repeated fascist ideology during the epoch of the Third Reich, decidedly *was* a fascist, meaning one adhering to and complicit with the policies of that regime, however distasteful that cognitive judgment may be and however complicated the term *fascist*.[18]

Having acknowledged serious discomforts with some of the positions of poststructuralism, I nonetheless regard it as crucial for rethinking the tasks of the historian in the present conjuncture. For the social formation in the advanced societies is increasingly characterized by discursive structures that are very difficult

to comprehend, such as computerized databases and TV adver-
tisements. These discourses are language formations with no
identifiable referents, representations without origins, discourses
that make their effects without resort to practices. And these new
communications structures, which are electronically mediated,
appear to constitute an increasing portion of the interactions in
everyday life. It may even be the case that such language formations are the stabilizing factor in advanced society, the element
that in some large part is responsible for short-circuiting efforts
at democratizing political change. Social communication has
changed from face-to-face speech to print, and now to electronic
mediation. Liberal and Marxist critical theories and their associated historical writings have assumed that print culture may intervene in oral culture in a way that leads to the elimination of
domination. In the present context of electronically mediated
communication, there may no longer exist enough oral culture to
support that relation. In short, face-to-face communities may no
longer occur with enough frequency and regularity to constitute
what was previously assumed to be a society.

In this context, it behooves historians to rethink the basic parameters of their framework, to recalibrate the registers of their
discourse to account for the new situation and then to reinterpret
the past differentially, in the manner of Foucault, in order to de-
familiarize and delegitimize the present. I offer the concept of
the mode of information as a step in that direction.[19] This concept makes use of poststructuralist theory because that theory has
gone farthest in moving beyond the assumptions about the relation of language and action that are embedded in liberalism and
Marxism and bespeak an earlier shape of society and because it
contains interpretive strategies that are capable of understanding
the power effects of discourses without reference to their alleged
material basis. Such an initiative in historical writing connects
with ongoing work in the new cultural history and in some
women's history. Of course, the older problematics of political
and social history are important to pursue. But the vitality of the

discipline depends on its ability to face to new issues and master new orientations.

Many historians respond to poststructuralist ideas as threats to reality. New theoretical protocols that I have shown are designed to increase awareness of certain dangers in the composition of historical works become somehow translated by historians into ultrarelativism. The mechanism of this transposition is that poststructuralism's linguistic turn is taken metaphysically: the analysis of the way language structures practice becomes for the historian a statement that language replaces reality. Sensitivity to issues of language structure become transmuted into an outright denial of experience.[20] In one of the more subtle considerations of this issue by a historian, Gabrielle Spiegel characterizes "postmodern thought" as "a flight from 'reality' to language."[21] Commitment to a metaphysics of language is attributed to Foucault and Derrida by eliding the difference between the structuralism of Saussure and Lévi-Strauss and *post*structuralism. In Spiegel's words, "As developed by semiotics and deconstruction, Saussure's investigation into the properties of language systems was to have disastrous consequences for a historical understanding of both textuality and history by severing language from any intrinsic connection to external referents" (p. 61). Yet a closer look at the work of Derrida, Foucault, and the other so-called postmodernists quickly reveals that they begin by rejecting the totalizing claims of structuralism and they do so, for one reason, precisely because such totalization (reduction of reality to language) installs the structuralist as capable of objective knowledge. Ironically, the historian and the structuralist are in agreement about the certainty of the truth, one seeing it as an attribute of reality, the other as an attribute of language. One does not begin to comprehend the postmodernists until one gives up these aspirations to certain truth. Instead, one must see them as metaphysical or even ideological obstacles to a critical form of cognition. The attention to language in Derrida and Foucault is an effort to avoid or minimize the metaphysical gestures of the historian and the structuralist.

Lawrence Stone, who highly recommends Spiegel's essay, names poststructuralism as the number-one threat to the discipline of history. Derrida and deconstruction regard texts, he writes, as "a mere hall of mirrors reflecting nothing but each other, and throwing no light upon the 'truth', which does not exist."[22] Derrida, Stone announces, in agreement with G. R. Elton (another fine reader of theory), is an "extreme relativist."[23] Stone attributes to all postmodernists the assertion "that there is no reality outside language," destroying "the difference between fact and fiction."[24] Many if not most historians regard the writings of Foucault and Derrida as denials that reality and truth exist, as evidence of an immoral relativism. But the fine archival work Stone has done on the family in England is threatened not by poststructuralism but by his own refusal of theory, disavowal of the role of language in his own texts, and blindness to the textual structurations of historical documents that contribute to *but do not in themselves constitute* an aspect of the past and the main pathway by which we access that past.

I hope that this chapter has provided at least an alternative if not a refutation of these views on poststructuralism by showing that its theory, far from denying that reality and truth exist, enables a more complex purchase upon them by promoting the *historical* analysis of the subject or modern individual. It provides the historian with procedures of self-reflection and categories of cultural analysis that help to preempt the blind projection of current figures of the subject into the past, that help to forestall the tendency of historians to erase the gap between the present and the past, and, above all, to foster a critical analysis of the naturalizing and universalizing propensities of current values and practices. The remarkable anxiety about poststructuralism displayed by many historians leads them to hurl wild accusations at it. These accusations are actually quite feeble and way off the mark. Anyone who has actually read works by Derrida and Foucault must find it quite amusing to see them berated for opposing truth and banishing reality. Once the debate between theorists and historians moves beyond this unproductive and uninteresting accusative mode, the actual challenges of poststructuralist writing to specific protocols of the historical discipline may be assessed and the question of new ways of doing history may be faced.

2

History at "the End of History"

As the twenty-first century approaches, the discipline of history faces a greatly altered landscape. The manner in which the profession defines the situation in which it finds itself and the quality of its response will no doubt seriously affect its future viability. If it misreads the historical conjuncture or if it responds in limited, defensive ways, its prospects will surely be diminished. I present this book to fellow historians with the intention of furthering a discussion about the conditions of a discipline confronted by new possibilities and alternatives. As far as I can determine, very little discussion is taking place, both within the academy and outside it, about the methods and topics of historical analysis in relation to a changing world. As a profession, historians do not reflect on the conditions of their knowledge production in anything like a systematic way and as a result, I fear, their work resonates less and less with general social and cultural concerns, because their assumptions and intellectual gestures connect less and less obviously with impulses of contemporary life.

The problem is how to define the changes in the context that are most pertinent to the discipline of history. Some commentators point to global political and economic trends: the disappearance of communism from Europe and that region's emerging

[handwritten margin note: caution to historians]

38

unification; the rise of strong economies in Asia; the shrinking size of the planet through improvements in transportation and revolutions in communication; the relentless deterioration of the ecology; the burgeoning of transnational corporations. Just as worthy of attention are the cultural and social changes: increased populations and their volatile geographic movements; vast gaps in the conditions of the wealthy and the poor; deteriorating urban centers and spreading postsuburban agglomerations; the disintegration of bourgeois, literate culture and its replacement by massified visual culture; the fragmentation of cultures in the advanced societies into an uncertain mixture of mutually hostile or indifferent groupings of fundamentalists, xenophobics, gangs, homeless, nostalgics, new agers, postnuclear families, and new social movements all encompassed by a commodification of even the least recess of the life world and its legitimation by greedy invocations of a mythic free market. Finally, academia itself is rocked by privatization under the euphemism "technology transfer," vocationalization, multiculturalism, challenging new technologies of teaching and research, interdisciplinarity, and a potpourri of methods and theories that many find troubling, even frightening. Lists of novelties such as these are easy to compose, but the question remains as to which items are substantial rather than ephemeral and which may serve to stimulate the formulation of new issues for historical investigation.

Not everything in the preceding paragraph of changes is either horrible or directly relevant to the discipline of history. Yet enough items are pertinent enough to evoke a spate of apocalyptic discourses about the end of history or the birth of postmodern society, issues that I shall discuss below. For the moment, however, I want to draw the reader's attention to one particular contextual novelty that I consider central to the renewal of discipline of history: the introduction, during the course of the nineteenth and twentieth centuries, of electronic systems of communication, from the telegraph and phonograph, to the telephone and radio, film and television, the VCR and fax machines, the computer and the Internet, and finally to the emerging integration of all these technologies. I shall argue that these technologies reconfigure the sense of space and time in a manner that calls into question basic assumptions of the discipline of history.[1]

The assumptions I have in mind concern the figure of the individual in the modern period. Modern historiography assumes a discursive author who is culturally situated in linear time and perspectival space. Modernity constitutes the individual in a horizon of time and space such that lawful causalities govern people, events, and things. Modern individuals may be characterized as rational and autonomous in good part because of their cultural imbrication with this configuration of space-time. Both the historian and the historical topics he or she writes about are inscribed in such scenes, fields, or narratives, and these are taken for granted as basic conditions of life.

Electronic communications systems drastically restructure this modern space-time matrix. In the words of Paul Virilio, "Point of view, the omnipresent center of the ancient perspective design, gives way to the televised instantaneity of a prospective observation, of a glance that pierces through the appearances of the greatest distances and the widest expanses."[2] Virilio characterizes electronic communications such as television as introducing simultaneity and immediacy, qualities of experience that reorganize the individual's sense of position in time and space. When one receives impressions via broadcast technology from Kuwait, halfway around the globe, as they occur and when, using newer technologies such as video conferencing on the Internet, one responds with the same instantaneity, then Euclidean space and linear time lose their credibility and cultural force. With the restructuring of space-time complexes comes a transformation in the general relation of human beings to machines. In these electronic communication systems, which are new skins of language, new wrappings of signification, an interface is constructed between the human and the machine that connects them and configures them in new assemblages. The old distinctions collapse: subject/object, living/dead, human/machine, inside/outside, observer/observed, sender/receiver. Again to quote Virilio: "The theoretical and practical importance of the notion of interface, that drastically new surface that annuls the classical separation of position, of instant or object [is changed] . . . in favor of an almost instantaneous configuration in which the observer and the observed are roughly linked, confused, and chained by an encoded language" (p. 52). With this altered cultural context the very conditions of being an individual appear as historically constructed and thus as a topic of historical investigation.

Agents versus Texts

With such new cultural formations spreading every moment to more and more social locations, having increasing influence on the identities of individuals, we may well ask how the discipline of history is to account for them and come to terms with them. Some evidence of the historians' response is found in their reaction to the theoretical development in the 1970s and 1980s known as poststructuralism. I shall review and criticize this reaction not to defend poststructuralism but with the aim of lowering the level of polemics and indicating how a more open attitude to recent cultural trends might benefit the discipline.

The salient position of historians in recent debates over poststructuralism is to defend the notion of agents over the theory of texts. They complain that poststructuralism (or literary theory, or postmodernism) reduces everything to texts. The notorious citation from Derrida, "There is nothing outside the text" (*il n'y a pas de hors-texte*) has become for many the rallying point of the defense of history. This statement proves, the argument runs, that all this theory stuff is bankrupt because it ignores experience in favor of discourse, dissolves agency into textuality, substitutes nihilism for social commitment. In Brian Palmer's words, "Critical theory is no substitute for historical materialism; language is

not life. . . . Left to its own devices, poststructuralist theory will
always stop short of interpretive clarity and a relationship to the
past premised on political integrity and a contextualized situat-
ing of historical agents within structures of determination."[3]
Palmer's Marxist complaint is fairly representative of most social
and political historians in its suspicion that poststructuralism
somehow occludes life, reality, politics. Just beneath the surface
of the raging argument lurks the hydra of moralism: history is
threatened, for these commentators, by dandies; ironists; overly
clever, self-promoting, irresponsible, careerist academic stars.
Actually, this defense of history attains little more than the conventional position of respectability. It is too easy to show that
Derrida in the above quotation does not mean that reality consists entirely of texts, which is surely not a position worthy of
much attention anyway. Instead, deconstruction privileges a certain principle of interpretation that it finds in what it constitutes
theoretically as "texts," for instance, as compared with "books."
It is also easy to show how disciplinary training in history systematically draws attention away from the obvious fact that historians produce a discourse or text and that they do so primarily
by performing operations on other discourses they call documents and, finally, that these aspects of disciplinary work are not
innocent trivialities but major characteristics of the kind of writing known as "history."[4]

Derrida's statement that there is "nothing outside the text" attempts to substitute his notion of writing for interpretive
schemes that pretend to have access to a full reality. The phrase
appears in his works first in relation to the interpretation of
Rousseau, where Derrida insists that the notions of "real life"
and "natural presence" are not suitable approaches. Acts of interpretation require a sense of distance from their object.[5] Derrida's
insistence on the separateness of the interpreter from the object
interpreted is the theme of the next appearance of the phrase five
years later in the context of a critique of idealism, the Hegelian
effort to center reality in the interiority of consciousness. Since

historians cite the phrase in order to condemn poststructuralism wholesale, it is worth reproducing it in its context:

> To allege that there is no absolute outside of the text is not to postulate some ideal immanence, the incessant reconstitution of writing's relation to itself. What is in question is no longer an idealist or theological operation which, in a Hegelian manner, would suspend and sublate what is outside discourse, logos, the concept, or the idea. The text *affirms* the outside, marks the limits of this speculative operation, deconstructs and reduces to the status of "effects" all the predicates through which speculation appropriates the outside. If there is nothing outside the text, this implies, with the transformation of the concept of text in general, that the text is no longer the snug airtight inside of an interiority or an identity-to-itself . . . but rather a different placement of the effects of opening and closing.[6]

Derrida's "nothing outside the text" is a critique of idealist strategies of marginalizing everything outside consciousness. Deconstruction introduces a materialist notion of differential textuality to save exteriority, the outside, the other from the pretensions of a colonizing concept of mind.[7]

In the defense of agency over texts, the historian attempts to preserve the unity and the validity of the *experience* of historical figures. This bespeaks the fine intention of celebrating the capacity of individuals to resist oppression and the historian's role in preserving the memory of that resistance. The historian does not want to be reminded that texts intervene between him/herself and the historical moment, that texts have multiple meanings, and that reading them is not only an act of decoding but also an interpretation, one that relies in part on the historian's own situation. Reminders of these complications may annoy some historians and appear as efforts to discredit progressive political positions, as trivial digressions from the giant task of preserving the memory of oppression so as to aid the project of emancipation. On the contrary, the insistence on the text is the only interpretive stance that is able to resist the hegemonic figure of "the individual," because only when the individual is understood as discursively constructed is the false naturalness of the modern, bourgeois individual disrupted. It may be paradoxical to some but it is nonetheless the case that critical historiography proceeds only by dispelling the view of the agent as the unified center of meaning. For this reason many antiracist and feminist critics have risked the dangers of "the linguistic turn" not in spite of but because of their commitments to radical politics.[8] Only by attending to the role of language can one comprehend the operations through which gender and race are socially constituted.

Instead of entering further into the epistemological and moral debate over the relative importance or intrinsic truth of text and agency for the discipline of history, I shall perform a historicist operation on these terms. I shall argue that one way to assess the merits of the two positions is to study the historical transformation of the context in which the terms are deployed, especially in the last fifty years. I contend that the importance of the poststructuralist attention to language for the discipline of history derives not so much from the logical value of the arguments of poststructuralists or from their demonstrations and exemplifications (although I regard these as largely successful) but from the trend toward the extension of textuality throughout social space, on the one hand, and on the increasing reduction of agency to a dim ideological hope, on the other. For what has occurred in the advanced industrial societies with increasing rapidity over the course of this century is the dissemination of technologies of symbolization, or language machines, a process that may be described as the electronic textualization of daily life, and the concomitant transformations of agency, transformations of the constitution of individuals as fixed identities (autonomous, self-regulating, independent) into subjects that are multiple, diffuse, fragmentary. The old (modern) agent worked with machines on natural materials to form commodities, lived near other workers and kin in urban communities, walked to work or traveled by public transport, and read newspapers but engaged as a communicator mostly in face-to-face relations. The new (postmodern) agent works mostly on symbols using computers, lives in isolation from other workers and kin, travels to work by car, and receives news and entertainment from television.

The new individual agent uses not only the telephone, radio, movies, and television but also computers, fax machines, copiers, stereos, portable music players, VCRs, remote telephones, and the Internet. All the second group have been installed in the home since the 1970s, a dramatic, even astonishing, reorganization of this space. The home has been segmented into multiple cultures[9] and even more significantly respatialized. Each home is now plugged into vast systems of symbolic exchange, interfaced with global networks of electronic communications. And as a result individuals are now constituted as subjects in relation to these complex information systems: they are points in circuits of language-image flows; they are, in short, *textualized agents.* Their perceptions are organized by information machines. Their sense of time is edited and recombined by systems of digitized sequencing: real time on tape, movies on demand, fast forward, instant replay, pause, slow motion. Their conversations are delivered by satellite, crossing the globe as easily as one crosses the street. Their knowledge is stored in electromagnetic archives that render reproduction literally immaterial, instantaneous, and, in principle, nearly cost free. Individuals who have this experience do not stand outside the world of objects, observing, exercising rational faculties, and maintaining a stable character. The individuals constituted by the new modes of information are immersed and dispersed in textualized practices where grounds are less important than moves. Certainly not all individuals are affected equally by these trends; there are disparities introduced by hierarchies of race, gender, class, and age. Such inequalities in the dissemination of textual agency need to be studied, heeded, and addressed politically.

Historians appear to me to be doing badly in the debate with theorists not because they are wrong in some objective or logical sense but because history has changed. The argument for the authentic experience of agents—the voice of the people—and the argument that the role of the historian is to represent of this agency no longer speak to the situation of individuals or groups in the advanced societies. E. P. Thompson's moving tribute to agency as authentic experience, while eloquent, has lost its critical edge:

> I am seeking to rescue the poor stockinger, the Luddite cropper, the "obsolete" hand-loom weaver, the "utopian artisan" . . . from the enormous condescension of posterity. Their crafts and traditions may have been dying. Their hostility to the new industrialism may have been backward-looking. Their communitarian ideals may have been fantasies. Their insurrectionary conspiracies may have been foolhardy. But they lived through these times of acute social disturbance, and we did not. Their aspirations were valid in terms of their own experience.[10]

Thompson's book, *The Making of the English Working Class*, became a model for U.S. socialist historians, who took it as a vindication of the working class today because it refutes the "condescension" of those historians who celebrate industrialization while ignoring its tragic costs. The "experience" of Thompson's obsolete artisans operates for these New Left historians to fortify the hopes for industrial democracy in the 1960s. But as Marx says, one must write history and struggle for freedom in relation to the circumstances in which one is born, and these circumstances have changed deeply and continue to do so whether historians recognize it, embrace it, or bemoan it. The past may become a coherent anchor of resistance or aid to critique only in relation to a given present and from its point of view. Can the past still serve as an arm of resistance? If so, what shape does this past have? What is the role of historical discourse in an age defined by altered, postmodern circumstances? Which past or whose past needs to be remembered in order to face more clearly the difficulties of today? How must this past be theoretically structured so as to make it an object about which knowledge can be formulated and produced? The issue is not whether it is possible to write a history of the conditions of the early industrial working class but whether it is pertinent. Is it not rather more important today to understand the early conditions of print and electronic communications and how these have altered the configuration of identity? If so, then we require theories that allow us to understand such cultural processes, theories that constitute the historical field around the issue of identity formation.

Tell the Truth

One of the few efforts to confront the issue of a postmodern history is *Telling the Truth About History*, written by three highly respected and rightfully distinguished historians, Joyce Appleby, Lynn Hunt, and Margaret Jacobs. I shall evaluate their endeavor to define the present situation of historical writing, to assess the ability of existing paradigms to cope with it, and to offer new directions for the discipline. My goal here is neither to praise nor to blame this book and these authors but to further the development of a critical historiography. Yet I must praise the authors once at the outset for taking up such an important task when so few others dare to do so. The vitality of the discipline of history, it seems to me, depends on serious engagements with important intellectual trends and consequent epistemological readjustments in research topics, curricular design, and writing strategies. The laudable aim of the authors of *Telling the Truth About History* is to "provide general readers, history students, and professional historians with some sense of the debates currently raging about history's relationship to scientific truth, objectivity, postmodernism, and the politics of identity."[11] They know full well that historians are woefully inadequate in examining the nature of their own discourse, the general traits of their own kind of truth. It is not at all unusual to find that professional meetings of historians include few discussions of the nature of historical truth.[12] Appleby, Hunt, and Jacob are fully aware of historians' limited response to these issues as well as the discipline's great theoretical deficit. Unfortunately, they are too quick to provide historians with an alibi for this shortcoming: "Professional historians have been so successfully socialized by demands to publish that we have little time or inclination to participate in general debates about the meaning of our work" (p. 9). This passage performs a very dangerous shift in the focus of the book, exonerating historians from self-reflexivity and setting into motion conditions for a limiting defensive posture with regard to "general debates about the meaning of our work."

The pressure to publish does not in itself exclude "general debates about the meaning of our work." One may publish exactly such works as Appleby, Hunt, and Jacob have done here. What hides behind this argument is the disciplinary rule against self-reflection, the injunction to produce works that add to the font of knowledge rather than question its worth. Language that suggests theoretical reflection, mentions or discusses difficult concepts from current debates, is generally regarded as inappropriate for inclusion in the texts of historians. In a debate with Dominick LaCapra about the value of self-reflective intellectual history, for example, David Hollinger grudgingly admits that it had some worth to histories of the canon of great texts but warns against the danger of trivialization and "loss of meaningful contact with the concrete" in purely methodological writings. Hollinger continues, "We then find ourselves talking about what others have said about what historians should do, and speculating about what might happen if historians followed this or that general approach. When we cross this perimeter, then, we move from 'discourse about discourse about discourse' to discourse about discourse about discourse about discourse."[13] If Hollinger's views may be taken as representative of the profession, the discipline has very successfully socialized its members to regard "general debates about the meaning of our work" as futile diversions from the "real" labor of gathering, sorting, and representing so-called facts. Yet when the context of historiographical production has altered, as I believe it has today, it becomes time to take stock. It may well be, as one commentator put it, that "the time has come that we should *think* about the past, rather than *investigate* it. . . . A phase in historiography has perhaps now begun in which meaning is more important than reconstruction."[14] The question of history's "truth" is now urgent, elevating self-reflexive writing, "discourse about discourse about discourse," into a matter of serious concern. Appleby, Hunt, and Jacob therefore deserve our thanks for boldly broaching the question of postmodernism and the current state of the discipline.

Historians have indeed been socialized by the discipline of history to avoid questions about the meaning of their own work. Any study of the nature of the truth about history must surely face the issue of what kind of truth historians produce and what mechanisms of self-criticism are built into disciplinary training. One might expect that a book on the topic of historical truth would raise questions about the validity and vigor of current disciplinary practices, that a major concern of such a volume would be a search for methods to evaluate disciplinary protocols. One might expect in fact that turning to a theory such as Foucault's discourse analysis would be a natural choice in this quest. In part, the authors do just that, arguing that Foucault and Derrida have much of value to teach the historian. But the brunt of their position is that external forces have reshaped the environment in which history is written and taught, that these external forces have an ambivalent impact on the profession, and, finally, that the discipline must preserve and conserve, as much as it is able, the standard of objective truth. The impression one gains from the book is that without the incitement of these external forces the internal protocols of historical work would not require examination. While I agree with them that external forces are bearing down on the discipline I differ from them over which forces are most cogent and, above all, over how they stimulate self-reflexive critique. While I regard changes in our context as opportunities for new research directions, Appleby, Hunt, and Jacob react, I believe, too defensively.

The title of the book, *Telling the Truth About History,* points to the subject very well: the question that needs to be asked is, what is the status of the knowledge produced in the discourse of history? Is this knowledge objective and universal or something less than that? Peter Novick's *That Noble Dream* demonstrated conclusively that historical knowledge has long been grounded in claims of objectivity that he characterizes as a "collection of assumptions" and "attitudes," including "a commitment to the reality of the past and to truth as correspondence to that reality; a sharp separation between knower and known, between fact and value, and, above all, between history and fiction."[15] Appleby, Hunt, and Jacob argue that this "absolutist" position about truth is no longer tenable and that Foucault and Derrida are the ablest critics of that stance and the surest guides to a path beyond it. At the same time, they reject what they take to be Foucault and Derrida's alternative to the absolutist position on truth—postmodernist relativism—seeking instead a new middle ground in the "qualified objectivity" of "practical realism."

The title of their book indicates the performative dynamics of the problem: that historical discourse is intertwined with power; that it has power effects; and that it is produced and deployed in a field of power relations.[16] For "telling the truth" is what our parents and grade-school teachers urged on us when we were children, as the authors perhaps are ironically hinting. "Telling the truth" was presented to us as a solemn moral duty. We learned that it is *good* to tell the truth, that truth is a moral as well as epistemological act. And we learned this lesson from people who had authority over us and were much more powerful than ourselves, people we loved and feared deeply. We learned that truth was good in situations where we had little choice but to agree. Further, we often learned this lesson in messy or ambiguous circumstances when our self-interest might have indicated otherwise: that the truth would hurt us or hurt someone we cared for; that the truth was another person's understanding of what happened that we were being coerced to adopt and repeat; that this same truth meant one thing to one person and something quite different to another. In these experiences, however understood, we were constituted as subjects who must tell the truth, as subjects for whom telling the truth is not simply an epistemological achievement but a moral and political one as well.

I do not know if the title resonated this way for the authors but their argument certainly gives precedence to the moral and political force of "telling the truth about history" over the properly epistemological level. Regardless of its epistemological value, truth is for them a *moral* goal: "We are arguing here that truths about the past are . . . worth struggling for" (p. 7). The problem with moral positions such as this is that they often hide or shield problems and uncertainties; they prevent certain questions from being brought into the open. The reader is coerced into consenting to the morally correct point of view as other positions are demeaned and presented in a bad light. In the case of *Telling the Truth*, historical truth is defended against the "cynicism" and "nihilism" of relativists who apparently attack it. The authors ominously warn the reader, "Every time people go down the relativist road, the path darkens and the light recedes from the tunnel" (p. 193). One dramatic line coursing through the book, then, is the moral defense of the truth against those who would relativize it. What is hidden by this moral posture, I contend, is the extent to which the discourse of history may itself be implicated in the state of affairs the authors wish to criticize. By externalizing the source of the problem to grand political trends (multiculturalism) and, in their eyes, questionable theoretical developments (postmodernism) they make it impossible to assess the extent to which the kinds of truths produced by historians are complicit, intentionally or not, with dangerous political and cultural conditions.

Telling the Truth is trapped in a deep ambivalence. Appleby, Hunt, and Jacob want to argue that recent democratizing political trends are positive and that the discipline of history ought to further such trends. At the same time, they assert that these trends undermine objective truth and promote nihilism:

> Our central argument is that skepticism and relativism about truth, not only in science but also in history and politics, have grown out of the insistent democratization of American society [the inclusion of workers, women, and minorities in the political process]. . . . We endorse the insights and revisions made possible by democratization . . . [i.e.,] healthy skepticism . . . [and] a multicultural approach to human history . . . but we reject the cynicism and nihilism that accompany contemporary relativism.
> (pp. 3–4)

The simple presence of large numbers of ethnic minorities in the classroom makes untenable Eurocentric and universalizing approaches to Western history. The discipline of history had been implicated in these repressive tendencies by its commitment to absolute, universal, objective truth. How then to rid the discipline of its Eurocentric epistemology but still maintain a posture toward the truth that is compatible with democratic politics? Here is the intellectual drama of *Telling the Truth*, the pivot of its successes and limitations.

The authors adopt a peculiar strategy: they argue that Derrida and Foucault best articulate a critique of Eurocentric "absolutist" knowledge, that Derrida and Foucault are postmodernists, and that postmodernism, drawing conclusions from its critique, goes too far in the direction of relativism and nihilism by reducing reality to language. To save history for democracy, the authors claim, one must depart from the postmodernists and return to a revitalized objective truth. While I agree with the first proposition, I disagree with the second and third. I shall take up these arguments in turn.

The label *postmodernist* for Foucault and Derrida is of course inappropriate in that neither accepted it and both no doubt would reject it. Derrida, for instance, explicitly rejects the label *nihilist*, a term Appleby, Hunt, and Jacob associate with postmodernism. In an interview with Richard Kearney published in 1984, Derrida responded sharply to the charge that deconstruction sees language as referring only to itself:

> It is totally false to suggest that deconstruction is a suspension of reference. Deconstruction is always deeply concerned with the "other" of language. I never cease to be surprised by critics who see my work as a declaration that there is nothing beyond language, that we are imprisoned in language; it is, in fact, saying the exact opposite. . . . I totally refuse the label of nihilism which has been ascribed to me and my American colleagues. Deconstruction is not an enclosure in nothingness, but an openness towards the other.[17]

But the labeling of Foucault and Derrida as postmodernist is not in itself a problem for me because the same demurrals have been made by the French thinkers in relation to the term *poststructuralist*, which I regard nonetheless as a valid and useful label for both of them. The difficulty with *postmodernist* is that, applied to these thinkers, the term loses its meaning as a designator of a new cultural trend or even a principle of social organization. By missing the chance to understand postmodern culture in particular as an important part of the contemporary conjuncture, one that relates to multiculturalism and therefore to the fate of democracy as the authors understand it, Appleby, Hunt, and Jacob fail to come to terms with the relation of history to these developments. Postmodernity becomes for them a series of intellectual mistakes, theoretical exaggerations, and ideological threats. If they understood postmodernism as a dominant *cultural* trend they might have had to bring into question certain habits of disciplinary practice. They might at that point find more appealing Foucault and Derrida's critiques of the absolutist knowledge produced by the *modernist* historian. For Appleby, Hunt, and Jacob want their politics of democracy along with their objective historical knowledge except as this requires to be updated for the needs and conditions of women and minorities. They have not examined seriously enough the crisis of the discipline produced by these changes as well as those associated with postmodern culture.

Appleby, Hunt, and Jacob raise several arguments against the postmodernists. The success of their project for a renewal of historical writing hinges on the strength of this critique. They claim first that the postmodernist "argument against the unified self . . . undermine[s] the premises of multiculturalism. Without an identifiable self [note the slippage from "unified" to "identifiable" self—do they imply that the only "identifiable" self is a "unified" one?], there would be no need to worry about differing cultures, ethnic pride, and battered identities" (p. 202). Multiculturalism for them depends on a unified/identifiable subject, on a grounded, essentialized notion of the individual as rooted in a tradition or culture. Yet many of the leading theorists of multiculturalism associate such a view of the subject with a wrongheaded, conservative stance. Stuart Hall, a founder of the Birmingham cultural studies movement, contends that only a nonunified concept of identity allows a proper understanding of "the traumatic character of 'the colonial experience.' "[18] He then defines identity in the language of Ernesto Laclau and Derrida: "Cultural identities are the points of identification, the unstable points of identification or suture, which are made within the discourses of history and culture. Not an essence but a *positioning*" (p. 395). The decisive issue for Hall and many other theorists of multiculturalism is that only a postmodernist understanding of the individual as complex, unstable, and constructed allows for a properly *historical* grasp of minority experience.[19] Only if the self is not already unified is its construction in history possible. The cultural-political mechanisms of this construction were the explicit aim of Foucault's writing in the 1970s. Appleby, Hunt, and Jacob play to unfortunate nationalist tendencies in some ethnic movements by their insistence on the self as unified. They also display an unfortunate ignorance of the state of the debate within multiculturalist discourse, a failing that is no doubt shared widely among historians, who assiduously avoid these theoretical discussions.

Appleby, Hunt, and Jacob next charge the postmodernists with a loss of will: "Postmodernists are deeply disillusioned intellectuals. . . . Postmodernism is an ironic, perhaps even despairing view of the world" (pp. 206–7). Postmodernists are portrayed as members of a white, male, European mandarin class whose historical moment has passed. Their somber ideas are reflections of social and cultural decrepitude, this position generally asserts. Certainly the writings of Derrida and Foucault are contemporary with the decline of working-class politics, the crumbling of European empires, and the emergence of social movements such as feminism and multiculturalism that do not take as their center the subject positions of white male intellectuals. Yet empirically both Foucault and Derrida (along with Althusser, Deleuze, Guattari, Lyotard, de Certeau, and many others) participated in radical politics, organized movements and institutions, and were quite active in world affairs. Among contemporary French intellectuals perhaps only Baudrillard exudes the weltschmerz bemoaned by the historians, although even here the case is arguable. The postmodernists do, however, critique the modernist view of the intellectual, with its claims of authority to universal truth, its pretension to discern the shape of human history, past and future, and its husbanding of "the truth."

Thus Appleby, Hunt, and Jacob are right to condemn the postmodernists for offering no vision of the future: "Postmodernism cannot provide models for the future when it claims to refuse the entire idea of offering models for the future" (p. 237). And they are right to characterize postmodernists as opposed to totalizing narratives: "Postmodernism attacks meta-narrative" (p. 232). Yet they fail to see that these self-imposed limitations on discursive forms are precisely correctives to the "absolutisms" that they themselves complained about earlier in their book. The postmodernists place restrictions on discourse at those points where, in the modern period, it has led into justifications of political power (Lenin's view of the role of theory in relation to the working class or the legitimation of the unified nation in the United States by historical writing, as Appleby, Hunt, and Jacob

themselves so ably demonstrate) or the cultural suturing of hegemonic identity (supports for the rational male subject). They do
not recognize the postmodernist strategy of substituting what
Foucault called "a specific intellectual" for the universal one of
the modernist past. The historians continuously make erratic
and dubious judgments about the postmodernists, displaying a
serious lack of understanding of the latter's work. For instance,
they accuse the postmodernists of opposing the narrative form as
"inherently ideological and hence obfuscating" (p. 232). "Obfuscating" suggests an opposite of transparency when instead Derrida and Foucault search for the way narrative structures the
meaning of a text without the promise of total clarity. Even
worse they banish the postmodernists from the house of history:
"In the final analysis, then, there can be no postmodern history"
(p. 237). This terrible gesture of exclusion forecloses the possibility that aspects of the thought of Derrida and Foucault might
prove useful or even crucial for a reconstruction of the discipline
of history or the development of a "new cultural history," a project once highly touted by Lynn Hunt. It also dismisses without
examination those historians who explicitly turn to these
thinkers for support.

The final criticism against Foucault and Derrida by the historians points directly at the question of "the truth." For Appleby, Hunt, and Jacob, notwithstanding their rejection of
epistemological "absolutisms," transparent knowledge of the
world is the only basis for truth: "If postmodern theories are
taken seriously, there is no transhistorical or transcendent
grounds for interpretation, and human beings have no unmediated access to the world of things or events" (p. 225). The historian must have, for them, a privileged position of observation
and on that basis establish the truth of the past. This is the nub
of the disagreement. If the historians are correct, then the critique of logocentrism or Western epistemology by Foucault and
Derrida would be superfluous, even a waste of time. Historians,
in their "unmediated" relation to events, need only busy themselves with recording the people's wrongs along with the

wrongs of the people. But Appleby, Hunt, and Jacob have already shown us that historians never have such a lofty perch. They have shown how American historians of the early nineteenth century, for example, eagerly and with the best (revolutionary) intentions produced "the nation" for the nation, happily excluding women, blacks, and native Americans. They have shown that historical writing has discursive effects that by no means reflect an "unmediated" relation to events. Thus their argument falls flat that Derrida and Foucault deflect historians away from producing truth toward examining the truths they do produce: "Were this version of postmodernism applied to history, the search for truths about the past would be displaced by the self-reflexive analysis of historians' ways of fictively producing convincing 'truth-effects' " (p. 227). What could be more "fictive" as a "truth-effect" than the sign of the unified nation in the early national period of American history in the writings of historians? And what could be more useful than a self-reflective analysis of this discursive production? The discipline of history, it would appear, is perfectly ripe for an extended period of "self-reflexive analysis" as it confronts the confusion of deep cultural transformations.

Appleby, Hunt, and Jacob misinterpret Foucault and Derrida's stance against totalizing discourse as a depoliticizing move when in fact it is an attempt to renew the work of critique. The strategy of the little narrative or detotalized discourse, the effort to decouple monographic works from grand narratives, is precisely an attempt to produce a truth that delegitimates modern cultural and social forms. Some cultural historians have already forged ahead in this direction, offering a microhistory that disrupts linear narratives. The effort here is to discover a form of writing that does not mimic the cultural presuppositions of the subjects being discussed, a sort of ethnographic alienation effect within historical writing itself.[20] This writing is only relativist if absolutism is presumed as the governing norm. Certainly microhistory, like Foucault's discourse analysis and Derrida's deconstruction, cannot claim unconditional objectivity, but it does assert claims of truth, conditional and finite, but truth claims nonetheless. What Appleby, Hunt, and Jacob fail to understand is that the strategic hermeneutics of Foucault and Derrida are not designed to discredit discursive truth but to fortify it by removing legitimizing, foundational gestures that undermine its credibility.

The issue of the excessive relativism of Derrida and Foucault can only be measured against the degree of change required in the protocols of the discipline. I suppose it would be pleasant to continue to espouse the same terms as in the past (objectivity, science, truth), if with a touch of skepticism; in Thomas Haskell's terms, to prefer "a sensible moderate" stance toward epistemological issues.[21] But the issue raised by the postmodernists and studiously ignored by historians is to reveal the true historicity of historical knowledge, not to show that it is therefore weak, relative, and insignificant: these are critical judgments from within the modern episteme of absolutism. The point of Foucault and Derrida's arguments against objectivist, mimetic, representational truth is that truth matters quite a bit and only a deconstructed analytic position can reveal the dangers it contains without completely falling back into them, which remains a hazard—the hazard, perhaps—of disciplinary discourse. Appleby, Hunt, and Jacob's strategy of colonizing the term *postmodern* with the figures of Derrida and Foucault and then criticizing their ideas by citing for the most part the work of writers such as Sande Cohen and Elizabeth Ermarth comes back to prevent them from contextualizing their own discursive intervention.[22] For we are indeed entering a period of cultural life that does not fit within modernist horizons, a postmodern period in that sense, one in which social life is precisely increasingly textualized, in which language undergoes the drastic rewrapping of the mode of information or electronic technologies. At this time the discipline of history needs new cognitive maps, new strategies of analysis, and new thought experiments, and it is very likely that the most profound and serious thinkers of the recent past—Foucault and Derrida—will be most helpful in this endeavor. The very charges the historians make against the postmodernists— linguistic determinism and the reduction of the social and nat- ural world to language and of context to text (p. 230)—are exactly our best bets (of course, not as formulated in the terms of the critique) for rethinking disciplinary protocols. The attack on texts in the name of agency becomes instead a search to make sense of world of textual agents.

The End

Historians are not shaken by talk of an end to history. For most historians history is a real sequence of events that will end only with the last gasp of the last human being. History and human- ity are coterminous. In a sense, the grounds for this position are impeccable. We may freely grant that human experience has a temporal dimension that may at any time be represented as his- torical discourse. And yet no one may care. Only in some cul- tures are such discourses regarded as significant. It is worth recalling that the kind of writing produced by members of the American Historical Association is a recent phenomenon—a century old—and may well not last another. The question I wish to raise then is not the end of history as an aspect of human experience but the end of history as a discipline. Arguments are being raised more and more frequently that the kind of writing done by historians does not address the concerns of the day, or that it is being done better by individuals trained in other disci- plines, or that it supports an outmoded and dangerous institu- tion: the nation-state. Should the discipline of history continue and, if so, on what basis? In order to respond to this question I must first clarify the issues of that other end, the debate over the end of history.

The question of the end has no doubt been raised from the be- ginning. Its recent incarnation is certainly animated by Francis

Fukuyama's 1989 essay "The End of History" and its expansion in 1992 into a book, *The End of History and the Last Man*, as well as by the general debate over postmodernity in such works as Gianni Vattimo's *The End of Modernity* (1985) and Jean Baudrillard's *The Illusion of the End* (1992). Leading practitioners of the main standpoints in the dispute over history and postmodernism have written major essays in response to Fukuyama: for Marxists, Perry Anderson's "The Ends of History" (1992) and, for poststructuralism, Jacques Derrida's *Specters of Marx* (1993). In reviewing this literature, one largely overlooked by the authors of *Telling the Truth About History*, I shall glean and sift arguments about the current state of history (has it come to an end?) in relation to the current state of the discipline of history (how ought it respond to the situation?) In other words, these debates may help to define the present conjuncture and in that way may have an important impact on determining the directions the discipline of history might pursue.

In what many might regard as a departure from his earlier work, Derrida's *Specters of Marx* evaluates Marxist theory and in so doing reviews Fukuyama's discussion of the end-of-history theme. Certainly the occasion of a conference on Marx in the spring of 1992 at UC Riverside, to which Derrida was invited to present a keynote address, helps to explain the shift of attention to Marx. But this interest may be connected as well to the collapse of East European communism and the demise of the Soviet Union in the late 1980s. It may also be linked to Derrida's concern with politics and related issues since the 1988 revelations about the early writings of his friend Paul de Man. Since that time, Derrida's UC Irvine courses—on themes such as friendship, the witness, the secret—as well as his published writings—on European unification and on Benjamin's *Moscow Diaries*, for instance[23]—suggest his increasing interest in world affairs and political theory. But none of this prepares the reader of *Specters of Marx* for Derrida's explicit pledge of allegiance to and avowal of affinity with Marxism ("of a certain kind"), with democracy, with the Enlightenment, and with the project of emancipation.

Over the years Derrida made clear his preference for these key-stones of the political Left. Yet his systematic avoidance of direct, propositional statements as contradictory to the spirit of deconstruction renders particularly dramatic his unambiguous declaration of allegiance.

As the reader might anticipate, Derrida elaborates in *Specters of Marx* what had surely been taken as a minor literary image by commentators on Marx—the figure of the ghost—into a central problem of historical materialism. The ghost, for Derrida, indicates a rich, provocative turn in Marx's discourse but also an opportunity partly lost or defeated by the persistence in his writing of logocentrism or ontology:

> Marx continues to want to ground his critique or his exorcism of the spectral simulacrum in an ontology. It is a—critical but pre-deconstructive—ontology of presence as actual reality and as objectivity. This critical ontology means to deploy the possibility of dissipating the phantom, let us venture to say again of conjuring it away as representative consciousness of a subject, and of bringing this representation back to the world of labor, production, and exchange, so as to reduce it to its conditions.[24]

Derrida boldly proposes to improve on Marx, to eliminate his "pre-deconstructive" limitation, to "radicalize" him and calls for "a new International" that will instantiate "a new Enlightenment for the century to come. And without renouncing an ideal of democracy and emancipation, but rather by trying to think it and put it to work otherwise" (p. 90). These dramatic gestures are warranted, Derrida argues, by several unique features of the historical context:

1. the existence of deconstruction as a tool of analysis that, he states, "has always pointed out the irreducibility of affirmation and therefore of the promise . . . of justice" (p. 90);
2. the massive existence of "violence, inequality, exclusion, famine" resulting in unprecedented oppression, starvation, and even extermination (p. 85);

3. the astounding centralization of power in the nation-state by dint of vast "concentrations of techno-scientific capital" (p. 85); and

4. the spread of "new tele-techno-media" that transform public space and politics, infusing them with "ghosts" or "the spectral" (p. 102).

Given this definition of the conjuncture, of the urgency of mass misery and the concentration of destructive power in state and corporate institutions, Fukuyama's celebration of the final victory of liberal capitalism appears worse than naive. And this is exactly how Derrida regards *The End of History and the Last Man*. For Derrida, Fukuyama first commits the scholar's sin of ignoring relevant texts concerning the question of the end of history.[25] Fukuyama is indeed ignorant of the fascinating discussion in France in the 1950s and 1960s of the very issues he raises today.[26] In addition, Derrida shows how Fukuyama confuses two versions of the concept of the end: the ideal and the fact. Is democracy as an ideal triumphant over the globe or is it so in fact? In the final analysis, Fukuyama emerges as a poor reader of the Hegelian tradition of the concept of the end of history and a poor analyst of the political situation of the present and the relative realization of anything like justice, so that his discourse is little more than a dangerous apology for the status quo. With regard to my earlier discussion of *Telling the Truth About History*, it is worth noting that deconstruction, or postmodernism, emerges in *Specters of Marx* as neither pessimist nor lost in texts, neither nihilist nor relativist. Derrida presents an analysis of the *context* and adopts a clear, although somewhat undefined, political position. Through the analysis of Marx's image of the ghost and the discourse of Fukuyama about the end, Derrida, as postmodernist, engages fully with the political issues of the day. One may object to the claims he makes for deconstruction as the basis for a new international and the renewal of a nonreligious "messianic" spirit that will serve as a political beacon in the new millennium and as the true inheritor of Marx.[27] But one may not accuse Derrida of cynicism, apoliticism, and the like.

A reading of *The End of History and the Last Man* largely confirms Derrida's judgment of its weaknesses.[28] Fukuyama infuses new energy into the cliché "glib generalization." He manages to combine Hegel, Marx, Nietzsche, and Kojève—thinkers scorned and thought dangerous by Anglo-American liberal and analytic traditions of thought—into a celebratory medley for the folk tune of U.S. capitalism and democracy. Under the cloak of the "speculative" tradition of continental philosophy, Fukuyama toots the fanfare of the end of history as the victory of Western ideals: "At the end of history, there are no serious ideological competitors left to liberal democracy."[29] The advance of science, the expansion of wealth, the collapse of communism, and the spread of democratic institutions and values denote, for Fukuyama, the achievement and culmination of "History" as a grand narrative or total theory, not, let it be noted, of "history" as the sequence of events that never ends (p. xii). Feminism and postcolonial theory are not even considered as possible worthy competitors to liberalism. Putting them aside and putting aside as well socialist visions and ecological standpoints—in short, granting the lack of competitors—by no means guarantees that new positions will not emerge in the future, that liberalism in any form is adequate as an ideological framework for the realization of freedom in the present context, or that such freedom or any substantial version of it has in fact been realized by any much less all societies.

What escapes Derrida's notice in Fukuyama's imagined narrative ending is an unbearable, unrelenting, and completely unself-conscious masculinism. There are no worthy competitors, announces *The End of History*, so the game is over and the game is won, as if world history were a football game. In order to decorate this crude, muscular position in refined garments of discourse, Fukuyama turns to Kojève's reading of Hegel's struggle for recognition, finding in it a "thymotic" competition for prestige, a prideful, willful insistence on self-worth (p. xix) that bristles with testosteronic overtones, which allegedly drive the engines of history toward the telos of democracy. The realization of democracy relies, he contends, on an "irrational" self-assertion of its value and a lusty struggle for the victory of that vision. With history concluded, a new problem emerges for "the last man [*sic*]": "*megalothymia* finds outlets increasingly in purely formal activities like sports, mountain climbing, auto racing, and the like" (p. 318). Fukuyama has apparently read not a single work of feminist theory[30] (he cites none), or he might have learned from some of this literature that his "end of history" is easily comprehensible as the end of the white, male metanarrative, the end of the heroic bourgeois epoch, and the emergence of a time in which nonthymotic types are able to maintain full agendas without filling time by auto racing. Fukuyama's celebration of the end punctuates more than anything else the era of unselfconscious patriarchy. For feminists the struggle over abortion and child care are history, and they are not over. If for Fukuyama there are no compelling political visions beyond liberal capitalism it may be that this is so only from the vantage point of the Western masculine imagination obsessed with the battle of nation-states. At the end of Fukuyama's history it is not clear whether one is to celebrate the victory over communism or mourn the disappearance of the struggle against it: masculine *thymos* now has nothing left to accomplish. Meanwhile, the effects of the enormous gains of the women's movement have not even begun to be felt as new forms of gender relations, family structures, and child-rearing patterns are being invented and put into place, transforming fundamental aspects of culture and society.[31]

The other great achievement of *The End of History and the Last Man* is the transformation of what might have been a crisis of U.S. liberal-conservative politics into a self-congratulatory festival. The disappearance of East European and Soviet communism and the consequent evaporation of the cold war (and what an awesome opportunity for thymotic release that provided!) opened the danger of a political vacuum: in this case the end meant the literal vaporization of the enemy. So much of U.S. political culture and economic success in the postwar era hinged on competition with the Soviets that their sudden, unexpected absence raises the threat not only of economic instability but of deep political disorientation. Instead of facing the consequences and possibilities of a political life without this ultimate enemy, Fukuyama provides a grinning, blissful comedic narrative; he writes the "Hollywood ending" of cold war history. His book is a distraction for U.S. public life faced with the prospect of self-examination and reevaluation on the occasion of the end of the cold war. Now that the resources and energy previously allocated to that struggle (whatever its legitimacy) are no longer needed, what shall be done with them, and what have we learned from the experience?

Fukuyama defines his theoretical accomplishment as the demonstration of "a coherent and directional Universal History of mankind" (p. xxiii). Like Hegel's owl of Minerva taking flight at dusk, Fukuyama inscribes his Universal History after the fact, at the end. The end of history as a struggle for recognition, a "thymotic" contest, a rise of democracy allows Fukuyama the luxury of asserting the viability of the perspective of a universal history. The worldwide victory of liberalism gives epistemological force, in his eyes, to the discourse of universal history. The argument of postmodern theorists, to the contrary, is that "the end" means exactly the opposite: it means that such long-range or total histories are *not* possible. Of course the end for the postmodernists is different from that of Fukuyama, but the contrast in reactions to the same periodizing gesture is worth noting: both characterize the present as an "end," but each draws very different conclusions.

The literature on postmodernism is now enormous and the definitions of the term various and contradictory. I have raised the issue here in relation to the discipline of history and the way postmodernism serves as a new context for its self-reflection. With that in mind, Lyotard's now classic use of the term *post-modern* as "incredulity toward metanarratives" is most pertinent.[32] If he is correct, it is no longer possible to do exactly what Fukuyama asserts he has done: to present a coherent view of the human past as a single story. Lyotard's argument is that changes in the nature, production, and distribution of knowledge (the use of the computer in particular) render incoherent the grand narratives of the Enlightenment, where human history is a single tale of the progress of freedom. Instead, justice is furthered if the principle of difference inherent in "small narratives" is legitimated. Rather than a march toward a monolithic culture of rational, fixed identities, what is emerging in history, for Lyotard, is a multiplicity of incompatible points of view, a tapestry of diverse subject positions. Fredric Jameson's equally classic response to Lyotard is that postmodernism is better understood as the "cultural dominant" of "late capitalism." In this way, he preserves the claims for a Marxist grand narrative while admitting, with Lyotard, drastic novelties in the cultural configuration of the present.[33] Both cases confront an end (for Lyotard, that of modernity itself; for Jameson, of modern culture only), but in neither case is history as such theorized as terminated. What characterizes the writing about postmodernism contra Appleby, Hunt, and Jacob is not a gloomy end of all things but a periodization and articulation of a beginning, that of the postmodern.

Many theorists have discerned difficulties with the postmodern position. Gianni Vattimo, for instance, points out that Lyotard's announcement of the demise of totalizing history is itself a totalization. In addition, the thesis of postmodernity is flawed by the contradiction that the periodization of the "post," signaling a new epoch, is a characteristically *modernist* intellectual gesture, heralding a new set of concepts in opposition to prevailing ones.[34] Yet for Vattimo there is a sense of a deep change, of a new experience of history as precisely an "end of historicity." Arnold

Gehlen prefers the term *posthistoire* for this perception that individuals no longer inscribe their own lives in a grand historical narrative the way the modern bourgeois once did, individuals no longer orient themselves and fix their identities in the tale of human progress.[35] The incredulity toward metanarratives is then not so much an epistemological critique of totalizing narratives as an empirical judgment about experience or culture or daily life in highly industrialized societies. At this point it becomes clear that what is at stake is not so much the nature of the past and the status of discourses about it as a change in the present and the consequent impossibility of maintaining earlier forms of discourse about the past. The postmodern antitotalizing totalization is thus less a contradiction than an expression of the paradox of present conditions of living, writing, and observation.[36] To enunciate the postmodern is to refuse the modern and at the same time to invoke a modern form of discourse.[37] Put simply, one cannot formulate a description of the postmodern without at least implicitly referring to the totality of the past. The discipline of history must then develop discursive strategies that detotalize the past while recognizing a moment of totalization in its own epistemological position.

Whatever logical traps are entailed in the postmodern thesis, all theorists point to the role of electronic information machines, the new technoculture, as a salient determinant of the end of history. In Paul Virilio's words, "We are in fact switching from the extensive time of history to the intensive time of momentariness without history—with the aid of contemporary technologies."[38] However regrettable it may appear to some, daily life increasingly includes electronically mediated communications that position participants or audiences in a space-time continuum that is discontinuous and simultaneous rather than linear, dispersed and ubiquitous rather than perspectival. These are cultural constituents of television, film, computer communication, and the rest, and they have already deeply transformed the characteristics of subjectivity of those exposed to them. This mode of information is spreading throughout the institutions of modern society and turning them inside out, making them postmodern.

In Koselleck's terms, historical time is generated by "the tension between experience and expectation which, in ever-changing patterns, brings about new resolutions."[39] Postmodernity is just such a new resolution of these constituents of temporality. Modernity (*Neuzeit*), Koselleck argues, constructs the pattern as a gap between past and future, a difference between experience and expectation in which what is anticipated diverges more and more from what has been. The future receives value as the past is discarded. In the premodern temporality of a "peasant-artisan world," Koselleck points out, expectations fed completely on the experiences of the ancestors; what was anticipated was what had already happened as the past pervaded the present.

If we look at postmodern temporality from Koselleck's framework, the present may appear to some to be a continuation of *Neuzeit* because technical innovations continue to orient experience toward the future. Yet a change may be said to have occurred: in the context of electronic communications the future is now. The present comes to be infused with the future, and the tense that best expresses the modern individual's historical sense is the future perfect, the future that has already been since it is embedded in the present. The distance between experience and expectation has collapsed as the present implodes into the future. One has a sense not that the future is imminent, a horizon that enables one to look both forward and backward, but that it has already happened. The linearity of modernity was sustained by the gap between past and future, a tension that gave the modern the sense of being propelled directionally, of forging ahead. In postmodern temporality, nonlinear and simultaneous, the future is here. In postmodernity, technical innovations do not serve to distance one from the past but to thicken an already subsisting technical world.

The academy in general and the discipline of history in particular are not immune from the effects of electronically mediated communication. Increasingly, written letters and even telephone calls are disappearing in favor of electronic mail, a technology that has its own parameters—encouraging spontaneity, for instance—which introduce changes in quality, not only in quantity or speed. In some disciplines, such as branches of physics, publication is now primarily in the electronic form, bypassing print. Although relatively uncommon in the humanities, numerous scholarly journals are published either first or only in electronic form.[40] In addition to communication and publication, the sources of research—archives, text, and documents—are increasingly being made available in electronic form. This again means instantaneous global access, altering forever the material conditions of doing research. But, again, this conquest of time and space incurs qualitative change as well. Researchers are equalized by being able to publish their own work, and canons evaporate as each researcher establishes his or her own archive, his or her own hierarchy of documentation. In addition, hypertext programs enable every reader to restructure the text by personalizing the pathways through it, rearranging the order of significance that was once materially inscribed in the book by mechanisms of tables of contents, chapters, paragraphs, indexing, and so forth. Each reader becomes in a sense an author. Also, the relation of the word to the image and the sound is changed with their general digitalization. Once in computer-readable format, words, sounds, and images are easily combined in the same work—or text—such as what now appears on CD-ROMs. The verbal culture associated with historical work through the mere material constraints of reproduction is becoming integrated with a visual and aural culture that has not even begun to be explored in academic work.[41] If these changes in the habits of research are not drastic enough, equally, perhaps even more, challenging innovations are beginning to be instituted in the domain of teaching. Distance learning is now being set into place within a communications infrastructure almost capable of real-time transmission of text-image-voice. In addition, a multitude of mechanisms have emerged in network technology—list-serves, bulletin boards, MUDS, MOOS, and WOOS—that enable easy interaction outside the classroom. In fact, the institutions of the classroom, the textbook, and the teacher are all open to deep transformations as a result of the new technologies. How then is history to be taught, researched, and generally disseminated under the new conditions? And are not these conditions themselves alterations in history that the discipline of history must account for?

These changes in the domain of academia are not merely incremental technical novelties but revolutions in the material conditions of scholarly production and practice. In this tiny region of contemporary society something radically new is in the process of formation. Restricting ourselves solely to this area we can see how ludicrous Fukuyama's announcement of the end appears. While it is true that the full implications of the innovations have hardly begun to be concretized into general practices and routinized in institutions (for that matter, these innovations have not ceased to be invented and introduced; more likely, they have just begun) so that a new vision of higher learning (a post-modern vision?) is not available at this time, the conclusion that nothing new is on the horizon is simply folly. What has happened outside the masculinist focus of Fukuyama is that the center of change has temporarily shifted from political and economic forms to cultural and scientific domains. Once these transformations have reached a critical mass of sedimentation, fundamental reorganizations of the economy and the political system are likely to follow.

The question of a postmodern politics and the question of history's place in a postmodern society need to be approached with as much openness and imagination as possible. The caution and backward-looking reach of Appleby, Hunt, and Jacob and the urge to announce the end in Fukuyama belie the enormous transformations that are surely already in process. A society with women's significant participation, much less equality, an earth in danger of serious ecological disturbance, a biosphere increasingly open to scientific alteration, a sociosphere bathed in electronic communication, a global ordering and ethnic intermixing of a depth never before imagined possible: in this conjuncture, this edge of a human reconfiguration, the discipline of history has a vital role to play not only in exorcising ghosts but in contributing to a cognitive mapping that envisions a new democracy.[42] The postmodern world will be one of multiple realities, virtual realities, little narratives, cyberorganisms, and nonlinearities. A conception of truth equal to such a world is required, a mobile and self-conscious epistemology conversant with virtual realities as well as social oppression, nondefensive and nonthymotic in spirit, gaining its foothold not in the period of the Christian religious wars, as Appleby, Hunt, and Jacob recommend,[43] but from the emerging adventure of the conditions in front of us.

3

Furet's Intervention

François Furet's *Interpreting the French Revolution*, which appeared in French in 1978 and in English in 1981, represented an important moment in the development of a new cultural history. It has, for a book by a historian, the unusual distinction of attaining considerable celebrity and having considerable impact on the field without introducing any new research. The book must be regarded as a very odd sort of work to emerge from a historian. One might consider it a book about method, like Marc Bloch's *The Historian's Craft* (1942) or Carl Becker's *Everyman His Own Historian* (1935), but it is not really of that ilk. Nor is it a book on historiography in the manner of Pieter Geyl's classic work *Napoleon: For And Against* (1947) or G. P. Gooch's *History and Historians in the Nineteenth Century* (1959), because Furet does not attempt to contribute to a comprehensive review of works by historians on a given topic, in this case the French Revolution of 1789. Nor finally is it a study of the philosophy of history either in the manner of E. H. Carr's eminently teachable *What is History?* (1961) or Arnold Toynbee's grand metanarrative *A Study of History* (1946).[1] Instead, Furet has written an entire book, mostly very critical, about works by other histo-

72

rians, and this sort of thing just is not done very often in the discipline of history. *Interpreting the French Revolution* sustains a formidable attack on one particular strand, albeit the dominant one for at least a century, of research on 1789. It mounts a furious onslaught on a most distinguished group of historians (Jean Jaurès, Albert Mathiez, Georges Lefebvre, Daniel Guérin, and Albert Soboul, among others) concerning what is arguably the most important single topic in modern world history. By way of contrast, Furet praises the contributions to the understanding of 1789 of Alexis de Tocqueville, a nineteenth-century belletrist but certainly not a trained historian, and Augustin Cochin, an early-twentieth-century right-wing historian. Transgressing every canon of disciplinary history, Furet, a distinguished member of the history department of the Ecole des Hautes Etudes en Sciences Sociales and one of its former presidents, the home of the renowned Annales school, intervenes in the way historians go about performing interpretations.

Such is at least the way I want to read the book. But it is also open to a directly political reading. Such a reading would argue that the book is not a work about history at all but about politics in France. And much can be made of this argument.[2] Furet's opening chapter, "The Revolution Is Over," signals a most political note. *Interpreting the French Revolution* may be read as a polemic against Marxism in French political culture or, as one reviewer put it, as a rethinking of the Terror of 1794 in light of the gulag.[3] In this reading, Furet's book is a critique of the way 1789 operates as an ideological pivot in the late twentieth century. To the extent that French national identity is bound up with the great Revolution, 1789 functions as a sign that contemporary political parties attempt to appropriate for their own ends. In particular, French Marxist parties, communists and socialists, maneuver to control the sign of 1789 with its message of egalitarian community, linking it with their goal of a collectivist mode of production. Thus for Furet, "The Revolution . . . is our contemporary history," and Furet would like that to change.[4] He would like to erase the sign of Revolution from the text of French politics, to uncouple his nation's identity from its past and thereby undermine one of the chief ideological strengths of the Left.

The political reading of *Interpreting the French Revolution* opens itself to a philosophical reading. To argue that the Revolution is over and to wish that it were not "our contemporary history" is a position very close to that of a book that appeared in 1979, only a year after Furet's: Jean-François Lyotard's *The Postmodern Condition*. For Lyotard also called for an end to the role of 1789 in contemporary politics by announcing his "incredulity toward metanarratives," one of whose chief versions was precisely the tradition of revolutionary politics as exemplified in 1789. Modern politics, Lyotard contends, is grounded squarely on the image of humanity struggling against domination, on the idea of human nature as autonomous rationality acting to unburden itself from unnecessary chains of oppression. No particular historical narrative better illustrates this grand theme than the events of 1789, and no body of discourse better connects the grand theme with the Revolution than the Marxist historiography of Jaurès, Mathiez, Lefebvre, and Soboul. If Lyotard is at least in this work the poststructuralist philosopher of postmodernity, then one is tempted to claim that Furet, in *Interpreting the French Revolution*, is the historian of that same politico-philosophical constellation. One also might say that Furet initiates for the discipline of history the theme of postmodernism, a history divorced from an immediate assumption of the revolutionary metanarrative, and further that he brings to the craft of history the theory of poststructuralism.

But Furet is not nearly as consistent nor as rigorous as Lyotard, and he disappoints his historical colleagues. A more accurate assessment of *Interpreting the French Revolution* is that it introduces aspects of poststructuralist theory, faintly gesturing toward it, and approaches something on the order of a postmodernist politics but that it remains, in the end, tied to the conventional rules of positivist historiography and the hegemonic tendencies of liberal politics. A less kind reading would argue that Furet appropriates the then-fashionable politics of the *nouveaux philosophes*, deploying the ideological caché of gulag to batter the Left's positions and the similarly glamorous theory of the poststructuralists to harass the Left's philosophical ground. I shall argue that Furet flirts with the new positions but cannot or will not go far enough in their direction to inaugurate a new historiographical trend. What is at stake in this reading of Furet are the conditions of possibility of a new cultural history, and what is most unfortunate for the discipline of history is that Furet corrupts such an initiative with enough conservative venom to abort its debut.

The Critique of Modern Historiography

In other writings on historical method, such as the essays collected in *In the Workshop of History*, Furet defends the classic Annales position against what it perceives as positivist narrative history. In the lineage of Marc Bloch, Lucien Febvre, and Fernand Braudel, Furet advocates history of the long term, studying the underlying structures of everyday life in their relative immobility and aspiring to a "total history" that multiplies the levels of analysis. In contrast to these hallmarks of the Annales method, Furet disparages the naive narrative historian who traces one event after another, "a somewhat lazy mode of writing history,"[5] without any analysis or conceptual statement of a problem. In Furet's critique, "Traditional historical explanation obeys the logic of narrative. What comes first explains what follows. Since history thus defined has a meaning that predates, so to speak, the set of phenomena that it encompasses, historical facts need only be arranged on the time scale to become meaningful within a process known in advance. . . . The model of this type of history is political history" (pp. 8–9). Against narrative political history, the Annales offered the alternative of history inspired by the methods of the social sciences, preferring "to analyze deeper trends rather than superficial change" (p. 9). In *In the Workshop*, Furet applauds Annales methods for their theoretical self-consciousness and epistemological superiority over narrative political history.

Ironically, *Interpreting the French Revolution* badly upsets this comfortable Annales self-interpretation. In it, the opposition between a naive narrative of events and a conceptual analysis of structure does not work. This is so for several reasons. First, Furet's topic is a political event, so he finds himself out of the familiar boundaries of the Annales paradigm of economic and social structure. Second, the historians Furet wants to dismiss are those who bring to the study of 1789 both the results of research on long-term social and economic trends and a conceptual apparatus (albeit a Marxist one), the very kinds of strategies favored by the Annales school. If he were to be consistent with the Annales paradigm, Furet would have to argue that the Marxist historians are the true narrative historians and that de Tocqueville and Cochin, Furet's preferred analysts of 1789, are the true social scientific historians. In fact, Furet does attempt this reversal, as I shall show below. But he has another alternative open to him: that is, to develop a new paradigm different from that of the classic Annales position, a paradigm of cultural history. One deep confusion in *Interpreting the French Revolution* is that it attempts both these objectives without distinguishing between them.

Furet's first task in *Interpreting the French Revolution*, then, is to show how political events, such as 1789, can be approached by the historian with the same theoretical sophistication that he sees the Annales model having attained in the domains of the history of economic and social structure. He does have his two historiographical models to lead the way. De Tocqueville, the first model, had shown how the Revolution was a continuation of earlier structural trends, that the centralization of power in the state that the Revolution advanced had begun long ago, under the Bourbon monarchy. For Furet, de Tocqueville had thus examined "objectively" "the real content" of the revolution (p. 142). Political history must eschew reporting the utterances and acts of participants; it must step back from the heat of contention and bring "concepts" to bear on the events, concepts that are based on a firm understanding of long-term changes in the structure of the state. Furet's other favored historian, Cochin, was also able understand political history from an epistemologically superior position. Cochin, Furet notes, "treats an eminently 'event-bound' [*événementiel*] topic in terms of a strictly conceptual history" (p. 195). For my purposes, it is not necessary to evaluate the substance of Furet's claims about de Tocqueville and Cochin but simply to observe the argument he makes in relation to their work: political history may be conceptually self-conscious, long term, and structural. The problem with the Marxist historians of 1789 is that these attributes apply only to their understanding of the economic and social conditions of the Revolution. When they discuss the political events themselves, the Marxists fall into a narrative, positivist mode that takes the views of participants as reality.

With his demand for conceptual history, Furet pries a lever between the historian and the past, refusing to permit an identification between the one and the other. The deepest problem Furet can uncover in the historiography of 1789 is the problem of identity: the national identity of France and the personal, political identity of the historians. For him, both are confused with the critical understanding of the Revolution:

> All those histories, which have bitterly fought each other for the last two hundred years in the name of the origins of their opposition, in fact share a common ground: they are all histories in quest of identity. No Frenchman living in the second half of the twentieth century can perceive the Revolution *from the outside*. . . . Surely it is time to strip [the Revolution] of the elementary significations it has bequeathed to its heirs, and to restore to it another *primum movens* of the historian, namely, intellectual curiosity and the free search for knowledge about the past.
>
> (p. 10)

Here we have the basic opposition that informs Furet's book: identification with 1789 versus the free search for knowledge. This opposition appears to reimpose positivism in a different guise from the version dismissed by the author of *In the Workshop of History*. Against the false objectivity of the narrative historians, Furet appears to propose a true objectivity of nonidentity with one's topic through the use of concepts.

Such is not the case. In fact, Furet waffles back and forth on this issue with no serious resolution of the problem. On the following page, for example, Furet warns the reader, "I do not claim that those conditions will at last provide us with historical *objectivity*" (p. 11). He is aware that the historian is too situated, too politically implicated, to attain a stance of neutrality. Furet writes, "There is no such thing as 'innocent' historical interpretation, and written history is itself located in history, indeed *is* history, the product of an inherently unstable relationship to the past" (p. 1). Yet just one page later, while he appears to continue his skepticism toward objective history, he also, and quite contradictorily, makes a plea for political disengagement as a central criterion of a new agenda for history writing:

> Changes . . . are indispensable to progress in the historiography of the Revolution. In fact, this historiography should be made to show, not its colours, but its concepts. History in general has ceased to be a body of knowledge where the "facts" are supposed to speak for themselves.
>
> Society and the profession assume that they [historians] possess the virtues of patience and objectivity. The discussion of their findings is a matter for scholars and scholarship only. The historian of the French Revolution, on the other hand, must produce more than proof of his [sic] competence. He [sic] must show his colours.
>
> (p. 12)

On one page Furet asks the historian to be objective; on the next he acknowledges the impossibility of that ideal. On one page Furet complains of politically motivated history; on the next he is aware that no one can be outside of his or her time. And at one point he goes so far as to compliment the Marxist historians because they show "that questioning the present can be helpful in interpreting the past" (p. 87).

Confusion piles on top of confusion in Furet's argument for a conceptually sophisticated political historiography. There is one place in the text where Furet makes a distinction that may resolve the antithesis in which he has trapped himself. This is when he specifies to a certain extent the heuristic value of the present for the past: "For it to be useful, however, the scrutiny of the present must remain just that, a questioning and a series of new hypotheses, not a mechanical and impassioned projection of the present onto the past" (p. 87). The conceptually armed political historian may bring to the past a set of problems from the present but not an unreflected advocacy or parti pris. Until this point, it must be noted, Furet has said virtually nothing that defines or elaborates what he means by "concepts." In this last passage he suggests they do not provide "objectivity" but are linked with "hypotheses" that are in turn linked with the historian's political position or viewpoint in the present. Here Furet provides a nuanced position that might provide a starting point from which a new kind of history might develop. Let me emphasize, however, that the position in question is by no means sustained throughout the book; rather, it is enunciated only at one location in the flow of the argument.

Furet carries this promising line of theorization one step further: he acknowledges a certain danger in abandoning the ideal of objectivity by allowing for "hypotheses" from the present. The danger is relativism: "But lest [interpretation] lead to complete historical relativism, to a concept of history as subservient to the demands of society, an illusory anchor amidst uncontrollable drift, it must do more than simply state the role of the present in the history of the Revolution; it must also be accompanied by an expertise, as precise as possible, of the constraints imposed by *our own* present" (p. 83).[6] This apparently simple antidote to rela-

tivism incurs more difficulties than Furet admits. Historians are
not trained for "precise" "expertise" in diagnosing the constraints of the present, so Furet's antirelativist inoculation would
require a major change in the discipline. Even more troubling in
Furet's formulation is the persistence of homage to the ideal of
objectivity, the continued theorizing of the issue through the binary objectivity/relativism.

Toward a Conceptual History of 1789: Against Empiricism

If the ideal of objectivity is both asserted and denied by Furet, in
the entire text he sustains one important level of questioning
that bears in important ways on the elaboration of the concept of
"the concept." This issue is at the heart of all empiricisms: the
knowledge value of the historical actor's statement of experience. Whereas Furet's political animus is against Marxists, his
chief epistemological animus is directed at the historian's tendency—a tendency not limited to Marxists but characteristic of
all empiricisms—to accept as the experience of the past what
historical figures state it to be, though of course only after these
statements are verified as actual statements. The axiom of experience is central to the historical discipline. One finds it as the
leading epistemological gesture in writings by historians of
every political stripe and every nation and at every level of analysis. The most characteristic interpretive strategy of the historian
is to locate the voice from the past and find passages in which
that voice utters the statement the historian is seeking. For
example, in *The Female Malady*, Elaine Showalter argues that
women's condition produced insanity as a form of resistance to
patriarchy and populates her history of insanity with statements
by women who proclaim exactly that.[7]

In the case of the French Revolution, the experience in question is one of a break with the past. Furet connects the experience
of a break with the theoretical problem of empiricism: "Any con-

ceptualization of the history of the Revolution must begin with a critique of the idea of revolution as experienced and perceived by its actors, and transmitted by their heirs, namely, the idea that it was a radical change and the origin of a new era" (p. 14). What is at stake for Furet is not simply the problem of defining an era, of analyzing a revolution or a methodological axiom of a discipline, but rather the question of French identity. The discursive effect of the historian's empiricist error folds into contemporary politics, providing a foundation for the stability of French national identity. To be French means to be close to the Revolution; the most French political party is the one that most closely represents the Revolutionary tradition. By implication, if this link were to be shattered, politics would be transformed. Ironically, this implies another break, another revolution, such that Furet's intervention in the continuity of the Jacobin tradition performs a task similar to that tradition, although by other means.

The critical history of 1789 must, for Furet, depart from conceptually specified problems rather than from the immediate consciousness of the historical participants, with their sense of a break, their consciousness of being an origin, of establishing a new epoch—in sum, their temporality. For him, what "characterised the revolutionary endeavour" was "the eschatological ideology of a 'before' and an 'after,' of the new and the old" (p. 159). If the historian of 1789 lifts this theme out of the past without any conceptual mediation, the revolution becomes a pure origin in the present, "a mechanism that justifies the present by the past, which is the hallmark of teleological history" (p. 87). One of the unique problems in the historiography of 1789 is the mirror effect of the historian's search for origins reflecting back the participants' sense of being an origin. Furet does not distinguish clearly between the registers of the historian and the participant regarding the question of origin. On the historians' side, the problem is that a pure birth becomes an explanation of change; on the participants' side, the problem is that the pure birth is a quest for legitimacy.[8]

Furet does not discuss Nietzsche's or Foucault's critique of the function of the origin in historical discourse. These thinkers developed a theory of origin as multiple or relative, not unitary or pure, as emerging in a "field of forces," not as an absolute beginning. Foucault's notion of history as genealogy attempted precisely to break the teleological character of most historical writing, its tendency to provide a direct link between the "originary" past and the present in order to legitimize the present as a continuation of the past. Rather than pursuing the disciplinary historian's search for origins as links, Foucault proposed to seek out in the past moments of difference or strangeness and, on that basis, to impose a temporality of discontinuity that would destabilize the present. What I find most regrettable in Furet's account is that he applauds this feature in the writings of Tocqueville and others but does nothing with it. He praises these historians for their "amazement at the *strangeness* of the phenomenon [of 1789]" but accepts their perception as limited to shaping "the existential purpose of their work as historians" (p. 84). He does not see that a critical history requires that this "strangeness" be the strategy of a conceptual analysis and the rhetorical result of the historian's discourse, not enclosed in the historian's "existential" consciousness. The problem of difference becomes central to Furet's critique of the naturalizing effect of Marxist interpretive modes. In the present context, it serves to underscore again Furet's failure to carry out the critique of empirical history by a full elaboration of what he calls "concepts."

Furet is especially happy with himself for noting a certain irony: that Marxist theory supports his antiempiricism against the Marxist historians. In condescending tones he writes, "In fact, one wonders whether . . . it is a great intellectual achievement for a historian to share the particular image of the past that was held by the actors in the Revolution themselves, and whether it is not a rather paradoxical performance for an allegedly Marxist historiography to take its bearings from the prevailing ideological consciousness of the period it sets out to explain" (p. 91). Having caught Marxist historians with their theoretical pants down, Furet further embarrasses them by indicating the Catholic Cochin as the one who proves to be the true Marxist. Furet continues:

> Cochin . . . shared Marx's conviction that men who make history do not know the history they are making and simply rationalise their role through mental representations that the historian must, precisely, subject to critical evaluation. In short, Cochin distinguished between actual experience and critical analysis of it, an all the more fundamental distinction as the revolutionary experience is characterised by a much more abundant output of representations and ideologies than are "normal" periods of history.
>
> (p. 170)

I shall discuss later the claim in this passage that the Revolution is a particularly inappropriate vehicle for empiricism because of its efflorescence of discourse. But now I must raise the related issue of theorizing politics as culture and the imbrication of this issue with the question of experience. The identification of Marxist historians with the Revolution raises a profound question about the humanism of modernity. The difficulty for Furet is that he wants to legitimize political history understood as culture, as values and symbols, but without relying on the historical actors who enunciated that very position. The Jacobins announced the possibility of human beings governing themselves based on their (innate) capacity for autonomous reason. They inscribed the value of reason as the basis for democratic politics, and they did so self-consciously. Furet writes,

> The Jacobin creed was indeed founded on immanence in history, on the realisation of values in and by political action, so that those values were at stake in every conflict, were embodied by the actors, and were discoverable and knowable as truth itself. . . . [The Revolution was] a kind of spontaneous equiva-

lence between the values of revolutionary consciousness—liberty and equality—the nation that embodied those values and the
individuals charged with implementing them.

(p. 29)

Furet wishes to upset this equivalence by proposing a new historical discourse that theorizes political culture against the
immanent consciousness of historical actors. Such history would
conform to the antihumanism of Foucault and other poststructuralists. Furet prefers to support his move not by acknowledg-
ing his debt to poststructuralists and theorizing his connection
with them but by looking to the past, to other historians, to de
Tocqueville and Cochin, for the legitimacy of his own interpretation. The success and the failure of *Interpreting the French
Revolution* hinge on this choice. In my view, Furet's reliance on
de Tocqueville and Cochin may serve him well with an audience
of empiricist historians but at the cost of seriously undertheoriz-
ing the new field of political history.

The Problem of the Level of Analysis

Furet translates his calls for nonpositivist, theoretically informed
history into an argument for a shift from a socioeconomic to a
political analysis of 1789. Again his account is a mixture of
insightful suggestions and conceptual confusions. He begins by
presenting what he considers the misguided paradigm of the
Jacobin-Marxist tradition of interpretation: the French
Revolution was "supposed to have given birth, simultaneously,
to capitalism at the economic level, to the preponderance of the
bourgeoisie in the social and political order, and to the ideological values that are assumed to go with those two developments"
(p. 19). Such an ambitious, multileveled approach has certain
affinities, at least in its comprehensiveness, with the "total history" of the Annales, an affinity that Furet chooses not to

acknowledge. The error of the Marxists, for Furet, is the manner in which they interrelate these several domains. Put simply, they impose a cause/effect logic that they export from the economic-social level, where Furet regards it as appropriate, to the political-ideological level, where he does not. He writes, "The French Revolution cannot be reduced to a simple cause-and-effect schema. . . . The main characteristic of the Revolution as an *event* is a specific mode of historical action; it is a dynamic that one may call political, ideological, or cultural" (p. 22). Furet's first charge against Marxist historians then is that they erase the particularity of the political.

The weakness of this charge is that far from being specific to Marxists, it applies equally to any socioeconomic interpretation. Marxist theory has a place for political action, especially revolution, which it sees as the outcome of the emergence of a new mode of production, elevating new social classes to wealth and power and stimulating new contradictions between classes. The Marxist position is not designed to illuminate political innovations, only to indicate their connection with the forces and relations of production. A problem arises only when the Marxist historian reduces the political to its link with the socioeconomic, eliminating other interpretive possibilities in a gesture of totalization. Furet, however, does not quite make this claim. He appears instead to argue the weak position that no socioeconomic interpretation can have anything to say about 1789, thereby reproducing the same totalizing gesture that he regrets in his antagonists. He writes, "These 'events,' being political and even ideological in nature, invalidate by definition a causal analysis based on economic and social 'contradictions' " (p. 23). Furet does not understand that theories open fields of analysis and suggest interpretations; they illuminate but do not control their field. Marxist history perhaps can say little about configurations of the political, but it is able to draw interesting connections between politics and socioeconomic changes.

Furet's second argument against the Marxist socioeconomic

interpretation is much stronger: that is, that it naturalizes the Revolution instead of indicating how it is a cultural construction. But here Furet's critique is directed not at any link between the mode of production and the events of 1789 but at the way the Jacobin/Marxists understand the revolutionary agent. Furet complains that "the Marxist vulgate . . . treats the most radically new and the most mysterious aspect of the French Revolution as no more than the normal result of circumstances and as a natural occurrence in the history of the oppressed" (p. 24). He later objects that this vulgate "makes 'normal' and obliterates what calls for explanation" (p. 51). By mounting this attack, Furet places himself, without proper announcement, in the camp of the poststructuralist critique of the humanist subject. The humanist historian views the oppressed as always ready to rebel, centered in their free, rational humanity, and burdened only externally by the chains that keep them down. This conception of the subject is a formula for dehistoricizing politics. Marx's view of the subject is too often of this type as, for example, when he refers to religion as the flowers on the chains of domination, implying that, if the chains and the flowers were removed, a fully free and rational subject would emerge. As poststructuralists show, subjects are not unified in fixed identities but rather constructed and reconstructed in historical conjunctures. Once again, however, Furet notes the problem of naturalization but does not go very far in unpacking its theoretical sources. Consequently, certain aspects of humanist essentializing creep back into his reformulation of the analysis.

What the Marxists fail to show, Furet contends, is the novelty of the revolution as a political innovation: "France was the country that, through the Revolution, invented democratic culture, and revealed to the world one of the basic forms of historical consciousness of action" (p. 24). Or in another formulation: "What sets the French Revolution apart is that it was not a transition, but a beginning and a haunting vision of that beginning. Its historical importance lies in the one trait that was unique to it, especially since this 'unique' trait was to become universal: it was the first experiment with democracy" (p. 79). The problem with these recastings of the interpretive issue is that they return squarely to empiricism or positivism. In these quotations Furet does not offer a new theory of politics or culture but only insists on the facticity of revolutionary politics. His move is to point to the past as an objective exteriority and claim "it was this, not that," politics, not economics. His half-baked theorization of the problem comes back to haunt him in the following crucial statement: "There is something in the concept of revolution . . . that corresponds to its 'experienced' historical reality, and is not subservient to the logical sequence of cause and effect: the appearance on the stage of history of a practical and ideological mode of social action totally unrelated to anything that came before" (p. 23). Sadly, we have come full circle, back to the "experience" of the participants, only this time in the guise of politics.

Furet does move beyond these limited repositionings, the exchange of politics for economics. He specifies the problem of the political innovation of 1789 not merely as a celebration of democracy but as an instability in the reinstitution of power. Furet accounts for the tendency of the revolution to destroy one regime after another, to "eat its children," as the result of its Rousseauian ideal of transparency and the structural requirement that, since a transparent community cannot be realized, this transparency must be represented. "Legitimacy (and victory)," he writes, "belonged to those who symbolically embodied the peoples's will and were able to monopolise the appeal to it" (p. 48). The "people's will," or Rousseau's "general will," is, of course, an invention, a political force that exists only in its representation. Since the representation of the people's will is at the same time its political presence, a struggle ensued over who occupied that unstable discursive position, events thereby moving from one regime to the next. The mediatory nature of the sign is the key to 1789: "The Revolution . . . ushered in a world where mental representations of power governed all actions and where a network of signs completely dominated political life. Politics was a matter of establishing just who represented the people, or equality, or the nation: victory was in the hands of those who were capable of occupying and keeping that symbolic position" (p. 48). At this point Furet has genuinely advanced a new theoretical problematic: in order to appreciate the political action of 1789 as a construction and as a logic, one must turn to language. He expresses the shift again as follows: "One of the most frequent misunderstandings of the historiography of the French Revolution is its attempt to reduce that dichotomy to a social cleavage. . . . That rationalisation of the political dynamic of the French Revolution has one major flaw, for in reifying revolutionary symbolism and in reducing political motivation to social concerns, it makes 'normal' and obliterates what calls for explanation: the fact that the Revolution placed that symbolic system at the centre of political action, and that it was that system, rather than class interest, which, for a time at least, was decisive in the struggle for power" (p. 51). When one makes the move to examine language, one shifts registers of analysis, and a theory of how to understand the register of language becomes indispensable. It is no longer possible for the historian to identify immediately with the participants of 1789 because language mediates that intervention and the logic of that mediation of language must become the occasion of a problem.

The Turn to Language

Unfortunately, Furet provides no theory of language, or its relation to politics, even as he insists on its centrality to the understanding of the Revolution. Reviewers have wondered about the ambition of *Interpreting the French Revolution* to produce a semiological reading of 1789. In her review of the work, Lynn Hunt captures well the distance between the aim and the achievement of the book:

Although Furet never identifies his own theoretical allegiances beyond an occasional reference to the young Marx and much polemical praise of Tocqueville and Cochin, he nonetheless concocts a fashionable blend of Foucault, Castoriadis, and Derrida. The key words are all here: *le discours*, *l'imaginaire*, representation, transparency, and the semiotic circuit, and they signal Furet's ambition to make sense of the great Revolution, so long associated with violence, hunger, and the conflict of the classes, as a fundamentally semiological event.[9]

While Furet certainly urges that interpretation shift toward language, he never offers the reader a coherent understanding of how language can work in the way he says it does. If the political struggles of the Revolution are semiological events, efforts to represent the general will, what is it about language that allows for such ambiguity, such a space of differences, and how is the historian to analyze the specific turns in political power?

The extent of Furet's insufficiency on this matter may be seen in his analysis of the victory of the Jacobins over the Girondins. His linguistic explanation reads: "The Girondins were . . . 'lightweight' . . . in their half-hearted use of the language of the Revolution. Robespierre, who identified completely with that language, could dispatch them in advance to a guillotine of their own making" (p. 68). Furet's so-called explanation is twofold: the Girondins were linguistically weak, and the Jacobins had strong intentions. Or, in another example from the next phase of the Revolution, Furet writes, "the Thermidorians . . . had wrested power from Robespierre by destroying his ideological instrument, which had been equality through the guillotine. Their own power could be preserved only through a shift in ideological commitment: equality through a crusade" (p. 71). These interpretive gestures are exactly the wrong ones to employ in a language-based account of politics. They presuppose an understanding of agency identical to what Furet criticized in relation to Marxism. In Furet's account of the changes from one regime to another, language is a tool for agents to use; the Girondins were not good at it, and the Jacobins tried very hard. These are Cartesian subjects, autonomous and rational with intentions and commitments, whose relation to language is entirely instrumental. Both Furet and the Marxists have humanist views of agency in which individual or group consciousness freely creates meaning and then acts on it. On the contrary, what needs to be shown is, first, What general features of language allow for a play of differences that opens politics to the movements of 1789? and, second, How does language actively structure the subjects who attempt to control it? Furet provides no hint of an answer to either question, and this is why Hunt is right to reprimand him for his insubstantial use of fashionable terms and references. Without a theory in answer to these questions the historian faced with the mass of utterances of the Revolution will regress to analytic moves that derive from the empiricism Furet wishes to transcend. And Furet himself has done exactly that.

Foucault provides a guide to the first question by understanding language as always imbricated with power. The couplet discourse/practice expresses this relation. Power is exercised through language, and language has power effects, specifically in constituting subjects. Furet recognizes the power of language to constitute subjects when he writes: "So the Revolution was not so much an action as a language, and it was in relation to this language, the locus of the consensus, that the ideological machine established difference among men. Ideology spoke through the Jacobin leaders much more than they spoke through it" (p. 178). In the Revolution the problem was to provide a linguistic vehicle that could transform the monarchy's subjects into the republic's citizens and to do so in a manner that would hide that very operation, making it appear natural. The construction of new identities could only be achieved in language through its capacity to interpellate or hail individuals, as Althusser argued, into their own misrecognition. Furet perceives Sieyès's pamphlet "What Is the Third Estate?" as being crucial to this process, but he misconstrues it, writing, "What could be represented [by Sieyès] was precisely what the citizens had in common, that is, the will to found a nation in opposition to the nobility. With that staggering tautology the new political world was invented" (p. 44). *Tautology* is a term in the constative view of language, claiming that the definition provides nothing new, only redundancies, in relation to the object represented. The power of Sieyès's oratory derives from another aspect of language, its performativity, its ability to hail its audience as already constituted in an identity that it is providing as it is being uttered. Tautology, if there is one here, is not a logical mistake but a form of power. Furet notes that the Revolution was characterized by a tremendous outpouring of discourse, a volubility that must be read by historians along Foucault's lines of constituting subjects.

Ernesto Laclau and Chantal Mouffe have gone furthest in translating a poststructuralist theory into the region of political analysis in relation to the second question posed above.[10] Language for them is also a matter of constituting identities, but they underscore the instability of the result. Individuals are always multiple and decentered subjects, they contend. Political power attempts "to suture," or to close, the indefinite process of constituting identities. Language is a suitable medium for this contradiction because words are different from things, having a somewhat arbitrary connection to them. Words or signs are empty to some extent, always needing to be filled by their referents, a link that must continuously be reproduced. Some signs are particularly volatile and open to negotiations and lexical struggles; these are ripe for the political arena. Articulation is the always tentative linguistic procedure of connecting signs and identities. For Laclau and Mouffe, the deconstructionist understanding of language permits a view of politics that avoids an ideological fixing of terms and identities, enabling a social constructivist alternative to a naturalizing of terms.

Furet begins his analysis of the role of language in 1789 by pointing to the rapid changes of regimes as a problem to explain: "There was an essential instability inherent in revolutionary politics, as a consequence of which the periodic confessions of faith concerning the stabilisation of the Revolution unfailingly led to renewed bursts of revolutionary activity." (p. 47). This instability was fueled by a binary opposition at the heart of the ideology of the Revolution: transparent democratic community, or general will, versus counterrevolutionary plot, or conspiracy of enemies. The Revolution had, by executing the king, evacuated power. The empty symbolic space was filled by the general will of the people. At the symbolic level, no material evidence of that will was possible in the same way that the king's body occupied it. The general will was a sign that remained empty and at the same time was exceeded. The only way the sign could be filled by a representation was if its opposite, the conspiracy, was also enunciated in relation to it. Thus the Revolution was trapped in a semiological bind: to give identity to the free community required the regime to give identity to its enemies. Of course, there were enemies, but that does not detract from the ideological problem of enunciating a transparent community. The instability of the Revolutionary regimes, at the linguistic level, derived from both the lack of material or institutional embodiment of the general will and the essentialist character of the general will, which attempted to fix the identity of the revolutionary subject.

The Revolution confronted the first problem with a great variety of political and cultural innovations, such as the festivals,[11] all of which aimed at legitimizing a new form of power by anchoring it in an imagined past. The second problem returns us to the deconstructionist theory of Laclau-Mouffe and the question of defining identity in language. Furet approaches this question in terms of an analysis of Robespierre:

> He alone mythically reconciled direct democracy with the principle of representation, by occupying the summit of a pyramid of equivalences whose continued existence was guaranteed, day after day, by his word. He *was* the people to the *sections*, he was the people to the Jacobin Club, he was the people to the national representative body; it was continually necessary to establish,

control and restore the perfect fit between the people and the various assemblies that claimed to speak in its name (above all the Convention), for without that perfect fit there could be no legitimate power, and the first duty of power was to maintain it: that was the function of the Terror.

(p. 60)

Fixing the identity of the general will of the people required *a cultural expression* of it, a point of enunciation and an act of enunciation. Robespierre served this semiotic function.

Furet unfortunately distorts his analysis into a weapon when he turns to condemn the process as ending necessarily in the Terror. To comprehend better the politics of the Revolution as a cultural process of identity formation, one would preferably forgo gratuitous antirevolutionary sentiment and concentrate on specifying, theoretically and empirically, the semiology of the process. A deconstructionist analysis leads not to a condemnation of the revolution by a self-appointed historiographical judge but to an appreciation of the cultural process of identity formation and the attendant dangers of essentialism. It leads, at least in the hands of Laclau-Mouffe, to a new call for revolutionary politics that would multiply points of enunciation and the constitution of identities in their instability. When Laclau cites Saint-Just ("What constitutes the unity of the Republic is the total destruction of what is opposed to it"),[12] he does so to indicate the tragic, authoritarian consequences of humanist essentialism as a cultural-linguistic mode of constituting subjects.

The Public Sphere

Despite Furet's limitations in developing a theory of political culture based on language, he does advance our understanding of the Revolution by investigating the linguistic preconditions of 1789 in the "philosophical societies." Relying on the research of Cochin, Furet substitutes for the Marxist historians' origin of

1789 in socioeconomic conditions, an origin at the level of political culture. If the democratic semiotics of 1789 was new, as Furet claims, it had its origins in a unique form of association that brought together the ideas of the philosophes with the sociability of the urban middle classes to construct a political culture of consensus.

> In the consensus of the lodges, the circles and the "musées" (cultural associations), one can already see the outlines of Rousseau's general will, the imprescriptible part of the citizen that cannot be reduced to his particular interests. . . . The philosophical society was thus the first example of collective constraint, and arose from the encounter between a sociological mechanism and a philosophy of the individual. The sum total of individual wills produced the tyranny of society, which was to become the religion of the French Revolution and of the nineteenth century.
>
> (p. 175)

Furet thus claims that in the matrix of the philosophical societies a new form of speech was born that was later taken over by the Revolution.

The speech in the philosophical societies was a new kind of language known as "opinion." Furet writes, "[The] world of political sociability . . . was founded on the confused notion called 'opinion' that came into being in cafés, salons, Masonic lodges and the so-called *sociétés de pensée*, or 'philosophical societies' " (p. 38). Jürgen Habermas has argued that such "opinion," or "public opinion," constituted a new "public sphere" not only in France but throughout Western Europe, a new political space that was to become the basis for liberal radicalism, as Furet argues, but also for a potentially universal form of democratic freedom.[13] Habermas sees in the philosophical clubs a union of the ideas of the philosophes and the conditions of not only urban social and economic life but in particular the comforts of the "private" bourgeois family. For Habermas, "The public's understanding of the public use of reason was guided specifically by such private experiences as grew out of the audience-oriented subjectivity of the conjugal family's intimate domain" (p. 28). In the clubs and coffeehouses, political conditions of equality merged with family conditions of private conviviality to produce a new discourse and a new subject: the language of the autonomous, rational individual. For Habermas, the critical use of reason was born in these discursive practices, a form of reason that he views as the basis of universal democracy.

Furet is not as optimistic as Habermas about the language of the public sphere. He agrees with Habermas that the discourse of the philosophical societies was politically radical: "What is new in the laicised version of revolutionary ideology—the foundation of modern politics—is that action totally encompassed the world of values, and thus became the very meaning of life. Not only was man conscious of the history he was making, but he also knew that he was saved or condemned in and by that history" (p. 52). And he agrees with Habermas that the dialogues in the clubs were oriented toward consensus: "For the purpose of the philosophical society was not to act, to delegate or to 'represent': it was to deliberate and to cull from its members and from discussion a common opinion, a *consensus* . . . [it was] a tool designed to produce unanimous opinion" (p. 174). But Furet does not find in the discourse of the public sphere the hopes of universal democracy of his German counterpart.

The first problem Furet notes with the philosophical societies as a basis for a new politics is their importation of ideas from the philosophes, intellectuals who were without power: "Men of letters assumed a function they could fulfill only in its imaginary aspects, that is as opinion-makers who wielded no practical power whatsoever. . . . [This] was to shape political culture itself" (p. 37). (Furet's Burkean distrust of intellectuals—academic masochism, it might be called—had some currency in France in the 1970s, but it could be applied with success equally to the legal training of most politicians in Western democracies.) His second concern about the philosophical societies has to do with the specific ideas they imported, that is to say, Rousseau's notion of the general will, as we have already seen. Third, and most significantly for us, Furet finds in the form of the discourse of the philosophical societies not the realization of critical reason but the "tyranny" of "collective constraint."

Although Furet's portrait of the public sphere is thus highly ambivalent, it nonetheless locates in the speaking situation of the philosophical societies a new form of politics, or "political sociability," which he defines as follows: "By political sociability, I mean a specific mode of organising the relations between citizens (or subjects) and power, as well as among citizens (or subjects) themselves in relation to power" (p. 37). Furet, it might be mentioned, notices even less than Habermas that the new political discourse was less than democratic in a number of crucial respects, among them the almost complete exclusion of women[14] and membership that, while less restrictive than other political institutions, was limited—in the case of the Masons, for example—to those of wealth and education.[15] In addition, Furet is oblivious to the influence of print on the new form of political culture. He might well connect his concern over the "constraints" of consensus to these egregious exclusions and important influences.

The problem of the public sphere as the instance of a new form of discourse also raises the question of the relation of the Enlightenment to the Revolution. In shifting from a socioeconomic to a political-cultural analysis of the origins of 1789, Furet is careful not to reproduce older forms of idealism. For example, he does not repeat the complaint, which goes back to Joseph de Maistre, that 1789 was the fault of Rousseau and Voltaire. In measured prose, Furet writes that Rousseau's "political thought set up well in advance the conceptual framework that was to become Jacobinism and the language of the Revolution. . . . Rousseau is hardly responsible for the French Revolution, yet he unwittingly assembled the cultural materials that went into revolutionary consciousness and practice" (p. 31). Learning from Furet yet disagreeing with his antirevolutionary animus, Roger Chartier, in *The Cultural Origins of the French Revolution*, reformulates the relation between Enlightenment and Revolution in equally careful sentences: "My preference . . . considers the periods of the Revolution and the Enlightenment as inscribed together in a long-term process that both included and extended beyond them, and as sharing, in different ways, the same ends and similar expectations" (p. 198). While these nuanced accounts of the relation of culture to politics are preferable to older statements of intellectual determinism, they remain insufficient in theorizing the linkage of language and politics.

Chartier, for example, explicitly sets out to define the level of the cultural, as distinct from the intellectual (p. 18). And, unlike Furet, he does not shy away from discussing the contributions of theorists like Nietzsche and Foucault to the problem of origins (pp. 4–5). He notes, for example, that the recognition of the place of language in politics calls for new forms of historical investigation and proposes "a different articulation of the series of discourse and regimes of practice. . . . From the one to the other there is neither continuity nor necessity" (p. 18). But, like Furet, Chartier does not connect the insights of the theorists to the historical examination of the question in any more than a perfunctory manner. He discusses, for instance, Kant's notion of the role of print in forming a universal public sphere, contrasting it with the face-to-face dialogic practices of the philosophical societies (p. 26), but says nothing about the issue of the transcendental subject constituted by print, the question of its presence/absence in representational forms of language, and its reinscription in an oral mode of communication in the philosophical societies. These discursive practices raise difficult theoretical questions for the field of cultural history. Ignoring them, Chartier is content to find a compromise position on the relation of culture to the Revolution, one that allows him, against Furet, to maintain a progressive politics and reaffirm the public sphere. He concludes,

> The omnipresence of politics imposed by the Revolution was thus not contradictory to the privatization of conduct and thought that preceded it. Quite the contrary: it was precisely the

construction of a space for liberty of action, removed from state authority and reliant on the individual, that permitted the rise of the new public space that was at once inherited from and transformed by the creative energy of revolutionary politics.

(p. 197)

The politics of representation in a transparent society, for Chartier, does not negate the autonomy of the individual in the private sphere.

But the wish to separate totalitarianism from the Revolution of 1789 does not resolve the dilemma of the role of representational language in politics. Furet's position, whatever its political drawbacks, takes us closer to a definition of the stakes of cultural history than does Chartier's perhaps more appealing response. The problem remains to articulate the kind of discourse introduced into politics by 1789 and to understand its particular tendencies toward domination, its restraints on freedom at the level of the constitution of the subject, as well as its role in the political dynamics of the revolutionary events. And finally these issues raise in turn the further question of the kind of historical narrative that can account critically for the cultural politics of the Revolution. To analyze the centered subject and its other, in relation to the semiotics of 1789, we need to look beyond Chartier and Furet.

Like Chartier, Keith Baker attempts to insert the problematic of language within a redefined field of the political culture of 1789. In *Inventing the French Revolution*, Baker offers an extensive discussion of the discursive origins of the Revolution, but unlike Chartier he is completely uncritical of Furet, positioning himself instead as a disciple continuing the work of the master. Baker also regards himself as a Foucaultian of sorts, arguing that the analysis of the political culture of 1789 depends on the category of discourse. Here is Baker's definition of political culture:

It sees politics as about making claims; as the activity through which individuals and groups in any society articulate, negotiate, implement, and enforce the competing claims they make upon one another and upon the whole. Political culture is, in this sense, the set of discourses or symbolic practices by which these claims are made. It comprises the definitions of the relative subject-positions from which individuals and groups may (or may not) legitimately make claims one upon another, and therefore of the identity and boundaries of the community to which they belong. It constitutes the meanings of the terms in which these claims are framed, the nature of the contexts to which they pertain, and the authority of the principles according to which they are made binding. It shapes the constitutions and powers of the agencies and procedures by which contestations are resolved, competing claims authoritatively adjudicated, and binding decisions enforced. Thus political authority is, in this view, essentially a matter of linguistic authority: first, in the sense that political functions are defined and allocated within the framework of a given political discourse; and second, in the sense that their exercise takes the form of upholding authoritative definitions of the terms within that discourse.[16]

While this definition of political culture turns appropriate attention to language, it functions to politicize language rather than to linguistify politics. Baker's "political culture" is a realm of language that is sensitive to the force or power behind and within phrases. It draws attention to the performative aspect of speech and writing insofar as the political position of the author affects how the words will be received. What Baker pays less attention to is the power of language, the rhetorical, structural features of a discourse as these enter the field of the political and reconfigure it.

Baker is particularly effective in destabilizing the concept of history in the field of politics. He analyzes various historical writings of the eighteenth century (those of relatively obscure figures such as Gabriel Bonnot de Mably, Jacob-Nicolas Moreau, and Louis Adrien Le Paige) to demonstrate how such writing is best understood as a disputed terrain in which collective identity is at stake. Baker writes "accepted understandings of the events and of the implications of the past constantly become subject to contestation, as social actors draw upon the powerful resources that these understandings offer in the service of competing

claims. . . . History, then, becomes the domain, not of discarded
memory, but of disputed memory" (p. 56). This is an excellent
formulation of the unstable nature of historical discourse. Such a
Foucaultian attention to historical writing as a political intervention in an agonistic field might also be applied to Furet's work,
and indeed to Baker's. Unfortunately, Baker makes no effort in
this direction, preferring to cast his writing and his appreciation
of Furet purely in a disciplinary framework, one that shies away
from self-consciousness about its own discursive effects.

Toward a Language-Based Cultural History of the Revolution

From the point of view of the theoretical problem of establishing a cultural history of the Revolution, Lynn Hunt's *Politics,
Culture, and Class in the French Revolution* goes considerably
beyond Furet and Chartier. In relation to the question of
Marxist historiography, her book is burdened by neither the animus of Furet nor the obligation to compromise of Chartier.
Instead, she clearly defines what a Marxist perspective can and
cannot do in relation to a cultural history of 1789. Since the
problem of 1789, she writes, "is not the appearance of a new
mode of production or economic modernization, but rather the
emergence of the political culture of revolution," Marxist history
is "not so much wrong in its particulars . . . as insufficiently dis-
criminating."[17] Marxist historians cannot distinguish in detail
which groups or regions participated in the Revolution in which
ways; neither can they analyze the kinds of evidence that would
further such a differentiated picture.

Also unlike Furet, Hunt unambiguously defines her project
as one of cultural history and her approach as a theoretically informed focus on language. She defines political culture in a manner that immediately points to linguistic evidence as the archive,
giving new prominence to bodies of documents and methods of
analysis that had previously been subordinate. She writes, "The

political culture of revolution was made up of symbolic practices, such as language, imagery, and gestures. These symbolic practices were embraced more enthusiastically in some places and by some groups than in other places and groups" (p. 13). And if these "symbolic practices" are at issue, then perspectives and methods of interpretation that can to decipher them are needed. She turns explicitly to poststructuralists and other theoretical positions that have been most used by literary critics but are appropriate to any discipline if language is the focal point of the analysis. Hunt announces with boldness what must be considered a controversial position: "I propose to treat revolutionary rhetoric as a text in the manner of literary criticism" (p. 25). For many of the current generation of historians, who turn without flinching to social science for methodological assistance but consider their discipline threatened by any hint of association with literature, Hunt's forthrightness must appear dangerous.

The danger, of course, is the threat to the boundary of the discipline of history, the boundary separating truth from fiction. When literary critics look at historical texts on 1789, they are not bothered by the boundary but feel compelled to take note of it. In a book on the rhetoric of the historiography of 1789, Ann Rigney duly notes "If we grant that all historical texts are signifying constructs, do we have no other option but to follow Hayden White in concluding that they are also 'verbal fictions'?"[18] The problem for Rigney is to get beyond the binary opposition set in place by the boundary between history and literature so that one may examine "what sort of 'signification' it is that historians produce and how they actually go about producing it through the medium of discourse" (p. xi). In this context, Hunt's interpretive strategy of subjecting the rhetoric of 1789 to literary analysis indicates that historians are beginning to produce, in Rigney's terms, new kinds of "signification." Hunt's strategy does not reduce Danton's speeches to Balzac's novels, but, at the rhetorical intersection of the two different texts, similar theories become appropriate as vehicles of analysis.

With a fresh point of departure, Hunt examines various "symbolic forms of political practice." She employs various theoretical systems to examine various bodies of "symbolic" evidence; in each case, she provides an explicit statement of the theory and then looks at an appropriate body of documentation. She invokes Clifford Geertz's concepts of "cultural frame" and "master fiction" to discuss the "imagery of radicalism," the resort to icons such as Marianne and Hercules to replace the king as a cultural center;[19] she discusses the theories of Derrida and Hayden White in connection with an examination of "the rhetoric of revolution." In each case, she is able to bring to light a level of meaning unavailable to historians who employ theories in which language is a transparent medium of expression. She can indicate how language was itself a level of meaning. In discussing various material symbols of revolution, such as costumes, calendars, and so forth, Hunt uncovers a productive function of language at the performative level: "Such symbols did not simply express political positions; they were the means by which people became aware of their positions. By making a political position manifest, they made adherence, opposition, and indifference possible. In this way they constituted a field of political struggle" (p. 53). Semiologically comprehended, symbols were a terrain of political emergence, a means of structuring political positions.

Throughout the book, Hunt is exceptionally sensitive to the performative quality of language, its ability to do things while stating them. Her analysis of the question of social transparency is a case in point. Furet merely bemoaned the ideal of transparency as a political disaster, one calling for ideological analysis but, in the end, simply a lesson to be avoided. Hunt takes as her starting point the "contradiction" of the revolutionary aim of transparency with the need for a "didactic" discourse to implement it. She writes, "While representing the new community, [revolutionary rhetoric] pushed toward the effacing of representation (in the name of transparency between citizens)" (pp. 48–49). To the extent that the revolutionaries required rhetoric to constitute the general will, it admitted that it did not exist. Hunt demonstrates that revolutionary rhetoric "was constantly subverting its own basis of authority" (p. 49). In her account, then, political culture attains a level of concrete analysis informed by conceptually explicit strategies of interpretation.

Even with the accomplishments of *Politics, Culture, and Class*, much remains to be done in the full development a historiography of the political culture of 1789. Despite the boldness of her departure, for example, Hunt remains shy of theoretical elaboration. Discussions of both Derrida and Foucault are thin and ensconced in footnotes (pp. 49 and 57), treated like embarrassing intruders in the pure flow of historical discourse. In addition, her fine analyses of the rhetoric and symbols of 1789 are not completely integrated with the second half of the book, on "the sociology of politics," which resorts to more conventional social-historical methods. This disjuncture is not necessarily a sign of failure, as Robert Darnton complained in his review,[20] but does indicate a kind of heteroglossia, or multiplicity of historical languages, one that needs to be theorized and accounted for explicitly. More experimentation and theorization will be required to explore the difficult problem of linking language-based cultural history with socioeconomic history. A related problem is the difficulty of redefining agency in relation to a new cultural history that persists in Hunt's text. She offers one of the more sophisticated formulations of agency in the literature on the Revolution: "There were structures or patterns implicit in the revolutionary process, but those structures were in turn shaped and transformed by the interaction between unself-consciously held political assumptions and self-consciously acting, socially embedded, political actors" (p. 219). Here Hunt articulates agency as a complex interaction between structural determination and self-fashioning. By this formulation she hopes to reconcile her linguistic analysis in the first part of the book with her socioeconomic analysis in the second. Yet she felt compelled at the outset of the socioeconomic analysis to repeat the humanist credo of the resisting subject: "The second half of this book proceeds from the supposition that people, especially people acting together, make culture" (p. 125). These two statements of the problem of agency do not add up very well, betraying historians' continuing resistance to the notion of escaping the metanarrative of modernity, the figure of the self-emancipating subject.

Finally, other theoretical models besides those of White and Geertz will have to be tested in the continuing analysis of the vast archives of materials of 1789, models such as those of Barthes, Foucault, and Derrida, to mention but a few. In all of this work the problem of the disciplinary boundary will have to be stretched, questioned, and redefined so that the embarrassment with which historians encounter the problem of language may become the occasion for an imaginative and serious working relation.

Toward a Postmodern Cultural History

Interpreting the French Revolution calls into question the basic metanarrative of modernity without pursuing the logic of its position in relation to a postmodern historiography. In addition to a limited conceptual development, Furet suggests little about what form of discourse a new cultural history might take. Philippe Carrard, in an interesting study of the discourse of the Annales school, is disappointed with the group's inability to translate its radical impulses into new forms of historical writings:

> If New Historians sometimes play games with their texts and their readers, these games are not radical enough to make the New History "postmodern" in the sense Lyotard has given to the term. To be sure, most Annalistes share in the current skepticism toward totalizing systems and the accompanying "metanarratives" which legitimize them. Their use of quotation marks with concepts like those of Marxism testifies to this loss of faith, as

does their [e.g., Furet's] indictment of such teleological scenarios. . . . But the New Historians' self-reflectivity remains directed toward the tools, whether methodological or linguistic, which they borrow from the outside. It does not apply, as in postmodern science, to the very foundation of the discipline, namely, to the "rules" which "validate" their knowledge. . . . They have not placed words like "evidence" and "archives" in quotation marks, nor have they questioned the principles that ground . . . the "documentary model."[21]

While Furet and other Annalistes have been highly critical of narrative history, they have done little to explore the theoretical issues that ensue from it or to experiment with new forms of narration.

At issue is the problem of explanation, specifically the linear forms of explanation that are characteristic of modern writing. Furet is equally unhappy with the causal model of explanation characteristic of Marxist socioeconomic history and with positivist narrative writing, preferring to substitute a new form of "analysis" for both. Yet Carrard's examination of Annales' writing uncovers a persistence of narrative (p. 37). If the modern metanarrative is abandoned, what form of narration should be substituted for it, and how will these new narratives avoid modern explanatory strategies? The metanarrative of emancipation and the teleology of freedom, characteristics of both the participants of 1789 and the historiographical tradition, contain strong explanatory protocols. Events are here fully accounted for and rationally intelligible either through causes or by a temporal narrative sequence that is unidirectional and irreversible. What is more, in the accounts of 1789, these discursive forms produce the historian as transcendent and objective, as the very same autonomous rational subject that the revolutionaries of 1789 thought they were constituting or emancipating. Furet's call for a new political-cultural history of 1789 raises these difficult issues without addressing them in any serious way.

In *Women and the Public Sphere*, Joan Landes provides one

model for a cultural history of 1789 that attempts to find an alternative to modern explanatory schemes and narrative forms, although I have space here for only a cursory glance at its implications for historical writing. Rejecting the masculinist dangers of causal strategies, she proposes what I would term a descriptive explanatory model:

> What follows is an interpretive essay in which I rethink from a feminist perspective, the decisive historical passage from French absolutism to bourgeois society. I argue that the shift in the organization of public life is linked to a radical transformation of the system of cultural representation. I do not offer a causal explanation, but rather an account of the way experience is organized differently in modern times.
>
> (p. 2)

Landes uncouples the connection between the metanarrative of 1789 and causal explanation by turning to the "weaker" explanatory model of description. But she also interrupts the explanatory power of narrative by presenting what might be called a nonlinear account of her subject. Her chapters are discrete studies that do not really follow easily one from another. She avoids inscribing a momentum in her text that would ground an origin of modernity in a unidirectional temporality. What opens up in her account is the space for the recognition of the other of the historiography of 1789, the history of women's role in it.

Landes accomplishes these important innovations in historical writing by highlighting the issue of gender as a disruptive force against both the participants' self-interpretation and some of the theoretical accounts of it, in particular Habermas's theory of the public sphere. Giving prominence to women as the marginal other of 1789, as the group that has no place in the political culture of the emancipated public sphere, Landes upsets the logic of universalist humanism. This interpretive move has its own danger of positioning women and a feminist perspective in the essentialist locus vacated by the male revolutionary. But Landes attempts to avoid such a recuperation by the nonlinear organization of her narrative. For Landes, then, a cultural history is possible if the theory and history of gender in the Revolution disrupt the modern explanatory strategy. The so-called origin of modernity in 1789 shifts from a triumph of reason and freedom, the assertion of an absolute beginning, to a more balanced story of victories over domination and the institution of new forms of domination, to a mixture of continuities and departures, with no clear subject holding a privileged, grounded position. In the development of a cultural history of the Revolution, a specific alliance emerges between a postmodern interpretive strategy and one based on the viewpoint of the other, the marginal, whether that of women, children, the poor, ethnic minorities, or some other standpoint.

4

Michel de Certeau and the History of Consumerism

The Problem of Cultural Studies

Of all the important theoretical writings in France in the 1970s and 1980s, Michel de Certeau's is the most germane to cultural studies. Cultural studies may be defined as an interdisciplinary, critical, historical investigation of aspects of everyday life, with a particular emphasis on the problem of resistance, that is, the way that individuals and groups practice a strategy of appropriation in response to structures of domination. The work of other theorists did not capture quite as closely as De Certeau's this specific blend of interests characteristic of cultural studies. Jean Baudrillard, for example, studies first the system of codes in consumer society and later the object itself (simulacra), dispensing entirely with the problem of the resisting subject.[1] Michel Foucault, to take a second case likely to be mentioned in this regard, wrote in the 1970s about technologies of power in connection with prisons and sexuality, attempting to specify their articulation without resort to an originary subject.[2] Only in a few essays written shortly before his death did Foucault begin to explore the question of critique as resistance, and even here the issue concerned the epistemology of the author more than the practice of everyday life.[3]

In the United States, cultural studies is often viewed as being in opposition to poststructuralism. Yet De Certeau's theory of cultural studies, as I shall show below, emerged from within his position as a poststructuralist. One finds in his writing the same congeries of themes and discursive moves that are evident in Foucault, Baudrillard, Lyotard, Derrida, Deleuze, Barthes, Bourdieu, and to some extent even Lacan and Althusser—in short, in the gamut of poststructuralist figures. Common to their work is a privilege given to language over consciousness as the point of intelligibility, a thematic of cultural issues as opposed to economic ones, a critique of the unitary authorial subject, a refusal of totalizing categories and positions of closure, a sense that a great period of history (modernity) is coming to an end and that something new though still not discernible is emerging. De Certeau's work reflects these poststructuralist themes but has a unique direction that brings him close to cultural studies as well: whereas poststructuralists generally shied away from the problem of resistance because of their reluctance to define the subject theoretically, de Certeau had no such inhibitions.

In this chapter I shall analyze the theoretical explorations of De Certeau with regard to cultural studies, reading especially *The Practice of Everyday Life*, *Heterologies*, and *The Writing of History*. In particular I shall examine the connection between his theory of practice and his poststructuralist thematics. I shall then examine certain works by historians on the history of consumerism, emphasizing those points where De Certeau's theoretical orientation might expand and deepen the parameters of historical writing on this subject. Specifically I am concerned with the question of the resisting subject as a theoretical and political issue but also as it relates to the writing of history.

De Certeau on History

None of the poststructuralists read the writings of historians as deeply or worked with them as frequently as did de Certeau. When poststructuralists engaged the historical discipline—as, for example, Foucault did—they characteristically defined themselves against and in relation to intellectual history, whereas de Certeau was especially concerned with social and cultural history. Foucault most often but not always viewed himself as outside the discipline of history and refused its titles; de Certeau did not. Both writers were equally opposed to the main tendencies of contemporary historiography—its realist assumption about the past, its totalizing frameworks, and its empiricism—but de Certeau engaged historical discourse far more consistently than did Foucault.

In the late 1960s Roland Barthes decoded the discursive operations through which historians produced in their texts a "reality effect."[4] The past "comes to life" in the pages of history books as a result of certain combinations of signifiers and referents. This uncanny metaphysical engine of historiography, this "reality" maker, is what fascinated De Certeau. How is it possible that a narrative form claims to produce not a fiction but a (past) real? How is it possible for a scientific practice and an institutional structure to constitute a type of writing that makes these conditions invisible to the reader? What peculiar kind of sustained, permanent ambiguity is it that historians practice, one by which a "real" past is taken for granted, another "real" past is represented in texts, and a "real" present is effaced from their production? The discipline of history, de Certeau writes, exists on a precarious margin:

> History would fall to ruins without the key to the vault of its entire architecture: that is, without the connection between the act that it promotes and the society that it reflects; the rupture that is constantly debated between a past and a present; the double status of the object that is a "realistic effect" in the text and

the unspoken element implied by the closure of the discourse. If history leaves its proper place—the *limit* that it posits and receives—it is broken asunder, to become nothing more than a fiction (the narrative of what happened) or an epistemological reflection (the elucidation of its own working laws). But it is neither the legend to which popularization reduces it, nor the criteriology that would make of it merely the critical analysis of its procedures. It plays between them, on the margin that separates these two reductions.[5]

The discipline of history thus bears a burden: it must deny that it is mere narrative, and it must refuse epistemological self-reflection.

Historians must insist that the stories they tell are not stories but truths, representations of past realities. But they must also spurn the prescription of truth to acknowledge openly its own assumptions, to lay bare its procedures to critical inquiry, to question its conditions of possibility. The trick for historians is to normalize a condition of writing that is anything but normal. De Certeau continues:

> Also thrown back either toward their present or toward a past, historians experiment with a praxis that is inextricably both theirs and that of the other (another period, or the society that determines them as they are today). They work through the very ambiguity that designates the names of the discipline, *Historie* and *Geschichte*, an ambiguity ultimately laden with meaning. In effect, historical science cannot entirely detach its practice from what it apprehends to be its object. It assumes its endless task to be the refinement of successive styles of this articulation.
>
> (p. 45)

The texts of historians are, for de Certeau, magical time machines, bringing the reader face to face with the past while at the same time denying the temporal gap that is being bridged. In a historical text one is *in* the past without mediations, with the words on the page disappearing as they are read.

The past as a form of reality, de Certeau contends, must be

maintained ambiguously as at once something beyond the text and something produced by and in the text. For the discipline of history there must be a real (the past) that the text must be able to represent. If questions were raised about research procedures having some active role in making the past or about present conditions inciting or motivating research on particular topics, then the bubble would burst, the ambiguous constellation would collapse. Thus historians do not, as natural and social scientists do, present their "theory" and their "method" before their "findings." For them only a "state of the studies" is permitted, and this simply demarcates the present work as an addition to previous works, a supplement to things left out of earlier accounts. Preferably, for historians, one begins right off with the factual narrative: on a certain day something happened. In this way we go into the real without the bad taste or impropriety of an epistemological apparatus.

De Certeau considers historiographical practice to be a form of "ideology": "History is entirely shaped by the system within which it is developed. Today as yesterday, it is determined by the fact of a localized fabrication at such and such a point within this system. . . . Denial of the specificity of the place being the very principle of ideology, all theory is excluded" (p. 69). This use of the term *ideology* is somewhat different from Marx's. The emphasis in de Certeau is not on an inversion of the real, nor is it so much a concern with the assumption of universality for the claims by a particular group. Rather, de Certeau wishes to call attention to the historians' disavowal of certain features of their practice and certain relations of their concerns with present conditions. De Certeau insists that:

> The "real" as represented by historiography does not correspond to the "real" that determines its production. . . . A *mise en scène* of a (past) actuality, that is, the historiographical discourse itself, occults the social and technical apparatus of the professional institution that produces it. The operation in question is rather sly: the discourse gives itself credibility in the name of the reali-

ty which it is supposed to represent, but this authorized appearance of the "real" serves precisely to camouflage the practice which in fact determines it. Representation thus disguises the praxis that organizes it.[6]

At this point de Certeau needs to indicate the material effects of this ideological moment on the practice of historiography, to demonstrate a possible alternative historiographical practice that would avoid this difficulty, and, most importantly, to resolve the question of how a nonideological historiography might be sustained without the ambiguity of the real as discussed above. If history is seriously affected by disavowing its conditions of possibility, and if a more critical practice is possible, what sort of a discourse would this new history be if it did not simultaneously rely on the assumption of a "real" past and a "real" produced in the text? Before addressing these issues, I must first examine de Certeau's analysis of the conditions of possibility that history occludes.

Archives, Numbers, Computers

De Certeau discerns several distinct levels of conditions for the possibility of a historical text, the disavowal of which presents different problems, and if they were to receive self-conscious recognition, different implications would ensue. First and most broadly, history, for him, is part of a "system," as shown above, a system at both the general locus of society and the particular locus of higher education. But de Certeau makes something unique of the classical Marxist move of placing discourse within society. To the extent that the monograph is produced within a certain social order, he insists, it is only one of many forms of history making within that order. History making goes on at innumerable dispersed points in the social space, places from which the discipline of history cannot completely sever its ties. Historical scholarship is not distinguishable from that prolix and fundamental narrativity that is our everyday historiography. Scholarship is an integral part of the system that organizes by means of "histories" all social communication and everything that makes the present habitable. The book or the professional article, on the one hand, and the magazine or the television news, on the other, are distinguishable from one another only within the same historiographical field which is constituted by the innumerable narratives that recount and interpret events.

(p. 205)

De Certeau here asks professional historians to acknowledge a family resemblance with journalists and everyone else who continually narrativizes, including friends and family, who make stories out of their lives, the lives of others, and the events of the world. This postmodernist refusal of the distinction between "high" and "low" history is an affront to the professional historian but reminds us all that the boundary of the discipline is guarded at a certain cost: that of misrecognizing the narrativity of historical discourse.

The second condition for the possibility of history, according to de Certeau, is the processing of records, the working on traces from the past, the reconfiguration of old writings into archives. The historians' craft, for de Certeau, consists in "transforming certain classified objects into documents. . . . Historians deal with physical objects. . . . They work on materials in order to transform them into history. Here they undertake a practice of manipulation which, like others, is subject to rules" (*Writing*, pp. 71–72). He underscores the active, epistemological function of writing history in contrast to historians' often passive self-conception as collectors of already constituted facts. The issue is not only one of bringing these "immense dormant sectors of documentation to life. . . . It means changing something which had its own definite status and role into *something else* which functions differently" (p. 74). Because language is a material mediation and not a transparent tool, historians need to acknowledge that they create facts by manipulating materials from the past, and they need to ponder all the implications of this creation.

If history is a form of narrative not different in principle from the myriad narratives found in everyday life, and if it is an active reworking of textual materials, it is, especially since the 1970s, an appropriation of one particular social technology: the computer. To the extent that the historian relies on the computer s/he is tied to the present, not the past: "The computer is inscribed in the historian's discourse as a massive and determinant contemporary fact" (*Heterologies*, p. 212). Yet the historian appropriates computer technology for the exact obverse aim: to lend objectivity and scientificity to his/her discourse, to remove the subjective component from writing, to lend authority to his/her text—in short, to produce truth, not fiction: "By the tribute it pays to the computer, historiography produces the belief that it is not a fiction" (p. 213). The computer sustains the fiction that history is that peculiar, almost oxymoronic phenomenon of writing: the true story.

What lies behind the historians' appropriation of the computer is the status of the number. Since the 1970s, the work of the Annales group in France, *Past and Present* in England, and the general turn to social and quantitative history in the United States, number has replaced narrative as the chief index of historical truth. For de Certeau, the danger of quantification is the illusion of objectivity it encourages: "Each book of history must include a minimal base of statistics, which both guarantees the seriousness of the study and renders homage to the power that reorganizes our productive apparatus" (p. 212). One might imagine that reliance on numbers would undercut the referential illusion of the historical text because numbers are clearly constructed by the historian. Statistical series are obviously produced by historians, not discovered, like some relic or diary. They are the result of operations performed by historians according to carefully determined mathematical protocols. But, de Certeau contends, the way in which numbers are received is quite different. They have only shifted the strategies of ideological misrecognition, changed the manner in which the historian has been able to secrete his/her operations. Like the early scientist Wilkins, historians would banish rhetoric from their language through the use of numbers: "At last [the historian] will be able to sever historiography from its compromising relations with rhetoric. . . . Thanks to the computer, he becomes capable of mastering numbers, of constructing regularities, and of determining periodicities. . . . Thus historiography becomes intoxicated with statistics. Books are now filled with numerical figures, the guarantors of a certain objectivity" (p. 208). Far from opening the way to theoretical self-reflection, the turn to numbers completely exonerates the historian from such annoying questions.

The real is now inscribed in the historians' text, de Certeau points out, by dint of the massive accumulation of numbers. Enormous data banks have been established to aid the researcher. With a few key strokes the historian may manipulate the archive with unprecedented ease. Size of information alone determines veracity and eliminates errors, historians believe: "The computation of large numbers will prohibit interpretations founded on particular cases or received ideas" (p. 211). If the quantity of cases is one guarantor of objectivity, another is the "univocity" achieved by reducing reliance on words: "One must define the units to be treated in such a way that the statistical sign (the numbered object) must never be identified with things or words" (p. 210).

For de Certeau, the historian's move to quantification is motivated by a fear of the instability of language, its polysemy. But this move simply displaces the problem of interpretation: now the units of analysis must be defined even more rigorously than before because quantification works more radically on the materials of the past than narration did. Quantifying social historians enact a more forceful intrusion into the archives than did their political historian counterparts a generation ago. The criterion of numbers drastically reduces the field of representation: through "statistical operation . . . one can retain only so much of the material being studied as is susceptible to arrangement in linear series" (p. 210). The theoretical task of defining one's analytic concepts comes increasingly to the fore as documents are reread through the grid of the number.

The problem of the construction of the field of analysis is particularly exigent because quantification enables new questions to be asked about the past, opens up research to new topics such as the family, women, consumption, and daily life in general. In comparison with political history, these topics bring to the fore questions such as what is an event? what is the unit of analysis? what is the field of investigation? Events are no longer acts of rulers but "combinatory relations of rationally isolated series" (*Writing*, p. 81). If that is the case, a question arises as to which units of analysis are to be subjected to this quantification; What constitutes, for example, an act of consumption? Or, again, what precisely is it about families or women that needs to be recounted? "The use of current techniques of information retrieval brings historians to the point of separating what until now was combined in their work: the construction of objects of research and hence also of units of comprehension" (p. 77). In the writing of narrative political history, the elements that compose the story appeared to be self-evident. In the social history of the 1970s and 1980s that was no longer so. Nevertheless historians did all in their power to use numbers as the answer to the question of the definition of the unit of analysis and to insist that this move required no theoretical justification.

Toward a Critical Historiography

Despite these enormous difficulties in the current practice of history writing, de Certeau kept his attention focused on that discipline rather than on literature (where Stuart Hall and the Birmingham school were developing cultural studies, in order to launch a new initiative in critical politics). History held a unique position in the emergence of a new politics because of its relation to the problem of time and its location at the border of "discourse and power." For de Certeau, the modern disciplines, including history, are characterized by a simultaneous totalization of time and neutralization of power. If these positions could be destabilized and possibly reversed, a critical discourse might emerge.

A salient theme of poststructuralist writing is a critique of the conjunction of the author as rational subject and the textual strategy of closure through totalization. Modern theory configures the author as a stable point of knowledge about an objective world and constitutes that world as a totality. In Hegel's case, to take but one example, the world is constructed as a totality through a process of becoming. Time is an unfolding of reality that the historian/theorist is able to know and therefore, in some sense, to control. Whether the world is Marx's dialectic of antagonistic classes or Weber's differentiation into spheres of instrumentality, its temporality configures knowledge and power in a unique symbiosis. De Certeau discovers traces of the modernist paradigm in the writing of history: "This 'globalizing' purpose is at work everywhere in the historiographical work. It ultimately refers to a political will to manage conflicts and to regulate them from a single point of view" (p. 92). The first step to a critical historiography, then, is to put into question the connection of time and totality.

For the modern historian, the figure of the rational subject of knowledge engages the question of discourse in relation to time. The split between the subject and the object is reproduced in historiography as the objectification of the past. The Cartesian project of knowledge/domination of the object receives its particular variation in the discipline of history in relation to the postulate of the past as outside, as the real. In de Certeau's words, "In the epistemology that was born with the Enlightenment, the difference between the subject of knowledge and its object is the foundation of what separates the past from the present" (*Heterologies*, p. 216). The historian maintains control over his/her object domain by constructing the past as an outside. Even though time provides the leading classifying procedure for the historian—periodization—it may not be problematized or thematized as a theoretical issue. This is the reason that Foucault's call, in *Discipline and Punish*, for a history of the present struck such a discordant note.[7] Thus the unacknowledged performative of history writing, for de Certeau, is the inscription of the other as the past, but an other that is thereby known and domesticated.

Critical history, like Foucault's, would reintroduce ambivalence in the relation of the past to the present. It would undermine the stable point of knowledge in the present in its relation to the stable domain of the past. At this point, de Certeau's definition of history—that it depends on the "fiction" of an outside (past) reality—begins to unravel. The reality effect of a historiography that calls into question the modern conception of time as an objective outside must be overturned in favor of some as-yet-unnamed other figure if it is to become critical. And yet just at this point de Certeau seems uncertain: is the postulate of reality a requirement of all historiography or only of its modernist mode?

De Certeau addressed this question only in part. He did so by evoking the subject position at the margins and thereby calling into question the rational, centered subject of hegemonic historiography. But the question of new temporalities and therefore of new figures of the real was not fully posed. Is it necessary for a new, critical historiography to presuppose a certain relation to an outside reality (the past), or are there different modes through which such a relation can be established, so different that the reality effects of their discourses translate into significantly different political effects?

Ideology, for de Certeau, is, as I have shown, the absence of place, the disavowal of the site of writing, the forgetting of the institutional practices that enable historiography. A new historiography of minority positions dissolves the ideological component of history writing, he contends, by insisting on the specificity of place and therefore the particularity of the subject position. In the following formulation he links critical historiography to the subject positions at the center of cultural studies: "That the particularity of the place where discourse is produced is relevant will be naturally more apparent where historiographical discourse treats matters that put the subject-producer of history into question: the history of women, of blacks, of Jews, of cultural minorities" (p. 217). In this statement de Certeau bridges the poststructuralist critique of the subject as author with the cultural studies' move to minority discourse. The historian of marginal groups is urged to question the authority of the rational subject and the neutrality, the placelessness, of this figure. Minority discourse opens the question of particularity, of a vantage point from outside, from a somewhere. This type of writing urges therefore the question of the subject as multiplicity and nonidentity. De Certeau explicitly writes, "The subject is constructed as a stratification of heterogeneous moments"(p. 218). Such heterogeneity for him raises directly the question of time: "Time is precisely the impossibility of an identity fixed by a place" (p. 218). In this way, the circle of his thinking about history comes to its ambiguous return: time as totalizing objectivity, the past as "real," corresponds to the historian as self-identical subject. Critical history upsets this theoretical gesture by introducing a move to the margins. At this point, the issue becomes one of theorizing the field of the everyday and its practices, with an eye to forms of temporality that contest the totalizing narrativity of the modern and its forms of historiography.

Times of Practice

In *The Practice of Everyday Life* de Certeau conceptualizes the field of a critical historiography. He defines the logic of practices in everyday life in light of their temporality, a temporality that maintains the ambivalence of the historian's position in the present while outlining a field of the past. In addition, this temporality is such that the identity of the subjects it defines will not be stable and unitary but fleeting and heteronomous: "Each individual is a locus in which an incoherent (and often contradictory) plurality of . . . relational determinations interact."[8] De Certeau's historical field is thus be populated not by individuals centered in rational calculation but dispersed and multiplied in a different sort of logic.

By moving in the direction of a nonidentical subject, de Certeau rebukes the traditions of liberal and Marxist historiography. For these latter positions the historical field of practice designates a type of agency that qualifies individuals and groups as full, unitary, and rational. The historian's task is to explain action in terms of a freedom that presupposes agency in this sense. Poststructuralists have been critical of this historiographical gesture because, for one thing, the subject it empowered mirrors the logic of modernity as the birth of rationality: the modern social system and the freedom of its populace faced each other in an abyss of resemblance. An instrumentally rational society and a free social agent were two sides of the same coin. With this problem in mind, de Certeau reminds his readers that his concept of practice is defined at the level of objective logics, not subjective intentions: "The question at hand concerns modes of operation or schemata of action, and not directly the subjects (or persons) who are their authors or vehicles" (p. xi). In this way, de Certeau attempts to avoid the trap of defining a type of practice that constitutes subjects in their identity, that constructs at a metaphysical level an agent—such as Robinson Crusoe or the Proletariat or the reasonable person of the judicial system—who will provide the historian with a foundation or ground for his/her narrative.

De Certeau approaches a very difficult set of issues: how to theorize for the historian a form of practice that connects historiography to an ambiguous relation of past and present and avoids projecting into the historical field the liberal-Marxist agent who is always already free, centered, and rational, inconvenienced only by an outside domination that, once removed, would allow a fully transparent socius to emerge. And de Certeau makes these difficult questions even more difficult by focusing on forms of practice that have lent themselves, in historical theory and writing, to confirming the binary of freedom/determinism. He theorizes, in short, the worst case of the self-identical subject: consumption. In place of the liberal historian's figure of practice as the heroic individual resisting political tyranny and the Marxist historian's figure of practice as the heroic group resisting economic exploitation and alienation, de Certeau theorizes the domain par excellence of nonpractice, the domain of passivity and inertia: everyday life, leisure, consumption, walking, cooking. Traditionally understood, these are not the sites of practice or action but nonhistorical spaces, empty time, waste. Indeed, at the hands of the Frankfurt school and so many others who have addressed the issue, this region of mass culture is a degraded world without hope or signification, a region so corrupted and baleful as to be virtually unintelligible. As Andreas Huyssen has shown, in these intellectual traditions, consumption and mass culture are, in a word, feminine.[9]

De Certeau defines consumption as the realm of the use of an object by those who are not its makers. But even in the realm of use there is a moment of production, of making, doing, or "poiësis," a moment of active re-creation. This moment comes into play at the gap between the received object and its appropriation. The model for what occurs is taken from language theory as the point of "enunciation." Like other poststructuralists, de Certeau has taken a "linguistic turn" in theorizing the social. The characteristics of the speech act, he argues, are those of the everyday, of consumption: "It effects an appropriation, or reappropriation, of language by its speakers; it establishes a *present* relative to a time and place; and it posits a *contract with the other* (the interlocutor) in a network of places and relations" (p. xiii). The question for de Certeau is, departing from a language model of enunciation, to develop a logic of consumption that neither reproduces the centered subject of liberal/Marxist theory nor bypasses the question of resistance.

He begins by turning to Foucault for a nonidentitarian view of social action. With a nod to *Discipline and Punish*, de Certeau wants to constitute the social field in terms of "the clandestine forms taken by the dispersed, tactical, and make-shift creativity of groups or individuals already caught in the nets of 'discipline.' " (pp. xiv–xv). In Foucault's sense, power is productive of subjects; it is a microphysics of discourse/practice, multiplied through social space, that evokes positions or configurations of subjectivity. But unlike Foucault, de Certeau will focus on "antidiscipline," on the moments of the turning or twisting of subject positions by consumers of technologies of power. He sees these as resistances that have been undertheorized and therefore marginalized even though consumer practice is "massive and pervasive," hardly a phenomenon of a statistical minority. De Certeau's gesture is here that of the leftist intellectual rescuing from obscurity a moment of social domination. He reinscribes this moment as one of resistance "from the bottom up," much like U.S. social historians who take as their model E. P. Thompson's *The Making of the English Working Class*,[10] but unlike them he resorts to a poststructuralist understanding of the subject.

The principal categories de Certeau elaborates to theorize consumption are "strategies" and "tactics." Once again, he opposes quantitative or statistical analyses because they reduce the active side of consumption to the appearance of passivity: "A graph . . . is substituted for an operation" (p. xviii). All the inconspicuous subtlety of consumption is lost in the univocity of numbers. To capture the "signifying practices" of consumption adequately, one needs a concept that can follow the nonlinear trajectories of the everyday. But "scientific rationality" generates concepts that impose on the social a grid of instrumentality, a "calculus of force-relationships." Like Habermas and the Frankfurt school, de Certeau is critical of those social theories that, deriving from Max Weber, visualize action in modern society only on the model of a calculation of self-interest. If society is seen as a field of strategies, a pullulation of centered subjects, each acting "rationally," as politics and economics are normally understood, the peculiar logic of consumption is lost.

Like a traveler in a strange land, the consumer, for de Certeau, brings a repertoire of practices into a space that was designed for someone else. The consumer brings otherness into society. The consumer inscribes a pattern into space that was not accounted for in its design. The art of such practices are what he calls tactics:

> Because it does not have a place, a tactic depends on time—it is always on watch for opportunities that must be seized "on the wing." . . . The weak must continually turn to their own ends forces alien to them. This is achieved in the propitious moments when they are able to combine heterogeneous elements (thus, in the supermarket, the housewife confronts heterogeneous and mobile data—what she has in the refrigerator, the tastes, appetites, and moods of her guests, the best buys and their possible combinations with what she already has on hand at home, etc.); the intellectual synthesis of these given elements takes the form, however, not of a discourse, but of the decision itself, the act and manner in which the opportunity is "seized."
>
> (p. xix)

Consumers are in this sense "immigrants," people who do not belong to the space they occupy. Instrumental rationality, by contrast, is sustained by the dominant institutions; its calculations mirror the hegemonic structures of power.

With the category of tactics, de Certeau extracts consumption from theories of mass society and repositions it as a form of resistance. Consumption is no longer victimization by the culture industry or irrational conformity to mass society but a play of heterogeneity, a disruptive intervention in the smooth operations of the system. Although late capitalism is designed for consumption, intended to solicit the infinite acquisition of commodities, the tactics of everyday life, according to de Certeau, continuously disrupt this logic even while confirming it—the housewife in the above quotation, after all, *buys the product*, which, from the standpoint of the capitalist, is all that really matters. Yet, although this is all that critical social theory has been able to see in such practice, with de Certeau, a theoretical shift occurs. His careful scrutiny of preparing meals, walking through cities, shopping, and so forth yields an alternative critical position. After all, try as they might, the social leadership has never been able to control these everyday practices in the manner of the Taylorist assembly line. No one can completely calculate, in some time-and-motion study, the preferences of consumers, even though everything is arranged to such ends: soft music, exciting lighting and displays, all the trappings advocated by contemporary market research. In this small gap between the world arranged by the hegemonic powers and the practices of individuals, de Certeau inserts his theory of consumption as tactics.

The theory of the everyday is surely no outline of revolution, no grand strategy of upheaval. Instead, de Certeau's position serves to confirm the unsutured nature of the social, the impossibility of the full colonization of daily life by the system, the continued fact of resistance to the temporal logic of democratic capitalism, and the ubiquitous eruption of the heterogeneous. His theory of consumption is an alternative both to the liberalism that bemoans the irrationality of mass culture and the Marxism that finds it always already controlled by the system. It provides a starting point for a type of cultural studies that is not predisposed to dismiss the billions of everyday practices in late-twentieth-century daily life but instead willing to discover in this heart of the beast a type of signification that might serve as a path through the thicket of modernity toward some future space-time conjuncture that might call itself postmodern. For historians, de Certeau's position promises to open a field of study that allies itself with other heterogeneous temporalities, those of women, ethnic and racial minorities, children, gays, and lesbians. To test the waters for such a project, I shall now look at an example of a history of consumption, evaluating it in relation to the proposals of de Certeau.

Historians Address the Issue of Consumption

In 1982 Neil McKendrick, John Brewer, and J. H. Plumb published *The Birth of Consumer Society: The Commercialization of Eighteenth-Century England*,[11] a collection of diverse essays with a provocative title. The title suggests a familiar gesture of historians: take a topic of generally recognized importance in the present and find its origins in the past. The mode of genetic argument—that a thing may be defined by tracing its origins—is doubled by the metaphor of birth. Logic and rhetoric are compounded in the title. But it also suggests another historians' ploy: to augment interest in one's period by identifying it with the present. Hence what used to be called "the ancien regime" is now "early *modern* society," a serious refiguring of the period 1500 to 1800 from one of difference (ancien) to one of sameness (modern). And now we learn that the eighteenth century, like the twentieth, was really a consumer society.

The Birth of Consumer Society is not only a redefinition of eighteenth-century England; it also initiates a new field for historians, that of consumption. Though certainly not the first book by a historian on the topic of consumption, it is among the earliest efforts. Historians who reviewed the book recognized its novelty. One reviewer deemed the book "a story . . . that . . . has been hitherto untold." She registered the book's innovation: "At a time when academic presses seems to grind out apparently endless variations on a theme, it is both astonishing and thrilling to come upon a volume on eighteenth-century England which breaks new ground. Such, however, is the gratifying experience granted the reader of *The Birth of Consumer Society*."[12] Other reviewers were equally cognizant of the book's innovative importance. One characterized it as providing "a firm foundation for future studies."[13] Another praised the book's accomplishment this way: "For . . . historians, a new world of inquiry lies before them—a new Pacific, waiting to be explored."[14] In general, historians received the book as opening a new field for investigation. Only one of the reviews by historians noted the problem that I shall address: the question of theory in relation to defining a field of empirical inquiry.[15] I shall pose this question in an analysis of *The Birth of Consumer Society* with an eye to the preceding discussion of de Certeau's theory of consumer practice.

In *The Birth of Consumer Society*, the general topic of England in the eighteenth century as a consumer society is discussed in Neil McKendrick's introduction and the first chapter, also by McKendrick, entitled "The Consumer Revolution of Eighteenth-Century England." The other pieces in the book, by Brewer and Plumb as well as McKendrick, are limited to case studies and secondary issues, such as the relation of consumption to politics and childhood. McKendrick's early contributions set the tone for the volume and delimit its field of analysis. They alone provide the argument that attempts to justify the title of the book, unifying an otherwise diverse set of essays that have in common only the fact that they treat the subject of England in the eighteenth century.

What, then, we may ask is a "consumer society," and how was it "born"? Both the introduction and the first chapter begin with bald assertions that propose to answer these questions: the introduction begins, "There was a consumer revolution in eighteenth-century England," and the first chapter begins, "There was a consumer boom in England in the eighteenth century. In the third quarter of the century that boom reached revolutionary proportions" (pp. 1 and 9). McKendrick characterizes a time and a place with the terms *revolution* and *boom*, metaphors that derive from politics and economics, and adds the attribute *consumer*. Up to this point, the reader does not know what the term *consumer* means, only that in eighteenth-century England there occurred a "revolution" and a "boom" of it. The next sentences in each chapter help the reader out: the introduction reads, "More men and women than ever before in human history enjoyed the experience of acquiring material possessions," and the first chapter echoes,

> Men, and in particular women, bought as never before. Even their children enjoyed access to a greater number of goods than ever before. In fact, the later eighteenth century saw such a convulsion of getting and spending, such an eruption of new prosperity, and such an explosion of new production and marketing techniques, that a greater proportion of the population than in any previous society in human history was able to enjoy the pleasures of buying consumer goods. . . . The eighteenth century marked a major watershed. Whatever popular metaphor is preferred—whether revolution or take-off or lift-off or the achievement of critical mass—[an] unmistakable breakthrough occurred in consumption
>
> (pp. 1 and 9)

These passages provide McKendrick's answer to the questions "What is a consumer society?" and "How do you know when it exists?" The answer is quantitative: a lot of buying goes on.

McKendrick defines "consumer society" in terms of liberal economic theory: a certain amount of demand in the market. The purpose of the book is simply to document this quantity of demand: "It will be one of the major burdens of this book to show that consumer behavior was so rampant and the acceptance of commercial attitudes so pervasive that no one in the future should doubt that the first of the world's consumer societies had unmistakably emerged by 1800" (p. 13). The particular variant of liberal economic theory invoked by McKendrick is Reaganomics, popular in both England the United States in 1982, when the book appeared. He adds a patina of ideological capital to his study by explicitly advocating the study of consumption for historians as an antidote to Reaganomics: "With so much evidence and so many arguments in favour of a consumer revolution . . . , one has to ask why so many historians have been so reluctant to proclaim their importance. The simple answer is that 'economic history is a supply side subject,' which takes market expansion to be a straightforward reflection of, and automatic response to, increased supply" (p. 30). Reaganomics' theoretical assumptions thus prevent historians from paying proper attention to consumption, a deficiency that McKendrick's book will attempt to correct.

But why was there such an increase in demand in the eighteenth century? The only answer provided by McKendrick is that there was a burst of innovation in commercial skills: selling techniques improved, inciting increased demand. This answer only pushes the question back one step: if one grants that commercial techniques improved, the issue remains why people responded so well to them, and here McKendrick says nothing, simply assuming that human beings, solicited in an effective manner, will want to consume commodities. Human beings, as noted above, have a natural penchant "to enjoy the pleasures of buying consumer goods." Thus liberal economic theory is invoked to constitute the historical field of consumer society without the least self-reflection. The only theoretical problem on the table is the question of the importance of consumption in relation to production. In de Certeau's terms, McKendrick has delineated the field in terms of "strategies," reproducing the instrumentally rational logic of capitalist institutions in the domain of consumer practices. And he has done so in a manner that disavows any dispute over his theoretical move. The only question he permits is the sibling rivalry of economic historians, one brother favoring production, another consumption.[16]

With the thorny theoretical issues safely tucked aside, McKendrick focuses on his chief concern: the empirical demonstration of dramatically increased consumer practice. It is a question of numbers. McKendrick treats the reader to a barrage of figures that purport to prove his point about a "revolution" in consumption. For instance, much more tea and printed fabrics were consumed in the period from 1785 to 1800: "While the population increased by 14 per cent in this period, tea consumption increased by 97.7 per cent and that of printed fabrics by 141.9 per cent" (p. 29). And this flurry of consumption must have been widespread through the ranks of society: "The rich simply cannot have drunk all the beer, worn all the cheap cottons, bought all the cheap pottery, buckles, buttons, and so on" (p. 29). These numbers stare at the reader with great epistemological authority, but, sadly, they do not dispel de Certeau's critique of their hidden rhetorical reductionism. For the numbers beg the question of their meaning. They function as characters in a narrative that are inserted in the story to produce verisimilitude. The "birth" (of consumer society) must have taken place because the signs of its presence are everywhere to be found. Yet the question of what or who has been born has not even been asked. Does purchasing a button in London in 1786 mean the same thing as doing so in 1986? Can we isolate these two acts from the web of institutions and practices at each of these two moments and conclude that they are identical? And is the act simply to be taken in the economic terms of a market transaction? None of these sorts of doubts furrows McKendrick's brow.

The matter of the birth metaphor also gives us pause. McKendrick resorts to it frequently in these brief thirty-three pages. In fact, he concludes the first chapter with a flurry of pediatric imagery:

> By 1700 the embryonic development of a consumer society had certainly begun, but the pregnancy had still some way to go. By 1700 the barriers to retail trade were certainly coming down, but there were still too many in place to prevent the protracted birth pangs of a nation giving birth to a consumer society from being seen to be over. By 1800, however, those barriers had given way and the consumer society had been announced by so many observers . . . with such a wealth of eye witness reports, such a mass of supporting evidence, that its arrival should no longer be doubted.
>
> (p. 33)

There is an important slippage in this passage in the narrator's use of the metaphor. From being a metaphor the writer uses to signify the qualitative social change toward a consumer society, the birth is presented as a past event that contemporaries witnessed. From a figure attributed by McKendrick to a time and place, it becomes fact. No one actually "announced" "the birth of a consumer society." The term was not used until much later. But McKendrick ascribes *past* truth to the announcement with "such a wealth of eye witness reports." In place of the theoretical work of elaborating the category of consumption, McKendrick uses the metaphor of birth and invokes witnesses to its reality. The historian need not do the theoretical work in the present because the witnesses from the eighteenth century testify to the birth in the past.

This is an egregious example of de Certeau's "ideological history." In McKendrick's use of the birth metaphor, the present situation of the historian is totally erased in favor of a representation of the past as real. All ambivalence about the times of past and present, all the space of the historian's disciplinary, institutional, and political practice vanish into air, all the discursive apparatus of the historian's metier dissolves as the empiricity of the birth replaces its theoretical problematization. Those outside the discipline might raise an eyebrow in wonder at the crude demonstration of epistemological innocence in McKendrick's text. I assert that it is typical, not a forced example, of prevailing disciplinary practice.

Agency Again

The worst consequence, perhaps, of McKendrick's "consumer society" is its failure to come to terms with the problem of agency or practice. McKendrick provides two versions of agency, neither of which is acceptable but both of which are commonplace in contemporary historiography. One is the entrepreneur as rational individual, the retailer who invents new sales techniques, who commercializes society on the ground of a presumed natural rationality, a given impulse to profit. This is, of course, the familiar autonomous individual who is the presumed agent of modern society and whose deconstruction has been a major goal of much recent critical theory. The second is the consumer, who also is presumed to have a desire for consumption, the very thing that ought not to be presumed. Contra McKendrick, a main concern for the history of consumption is the comprehension of the construction of consumer practices, the question of how the consumer subject was constituted. The desire for consumption is precisely what is in question and open for theoretically informed historical investigation.

De Certeau has contributed to this project by providing a logic of tactics that begins to make everyday practices intelligible from the side of the individual agent. He shows how the study of the agent's point of view need not assume as attributes of the agent those qualities that need to be investigated as historical constructs, how the desire for consumption, for example, may be understood as a complex tactic of a situated individual, not as a fixed aspect of human identity. This perspective complements that of Foucault, who studied the issue from the side of the object, the "technologies of power" that act on the subject, positioning her/him so as to be capable of consumer practice. Foucault's work intentionally omitted the response of agents to discourse/practices for fear of reintroducing the essentialized subject that he bemoaned in liberal and Marxist positions. De Certeau's work thus is crucial for historians who are open to Foucaultian theory precisely because it speaks to its greatest weakness.

But even with de Certeau's work, much more will need to be done both theoretically and empirically before an adequate history of consumption, a cultural studies of consumption, will be before us. For one thing, de Certeau's theory of consumption as tactics is not itself historical: it does not periodize different types of tactics, for example, those of modern society, of early modern society, and perhaps of postmodern society. Historical categories must have periodized variations before they can be appropriated for particular investigations. In Marxism, variations of class relations to means of production provide such complexity. In de Certeau, I find no similar elaboration. Second, the theory of tactics does not theorize the relation between tactics such as consumption to the politics of marginal groups. How are tactics structurally different among dominant versus subordinate positions? Or, as de Certeau's position currently posits, are all consumer tactics automatically those of the margin? Some work needs to be done to clarify more precisely than does the present formulation the relation of marginality in consumption and in movements among marginal groups that have explicit protest characteristics. Third, de Certeau does not bring together the two great areas of his writing about history. These are the issues of general epistemology and consumption as a particular practice. He does not theorize the question, in short, of the reality effect of the critical historiography of the everyday. How does a history of consumption informed by the theory of tactics avoid the historians' failing of denying their own conditions of production, presuming the real as referent, and discursively producing the real as an unintended effect of their writing? The answer to these issues might further a productive encounter between de Certeau's position and that of cultural studies.

5

The Future According to Foucault

The Archeology of Knowledge and Intellectual History

Judged as a discipline with coherent standards, methods, and problems, intellectual history would not place high on many scholars' lists. The field includes a disparate array of practitioners. Some prefer the style of Arthur O. Lovejoy and search for shifting configurations of eternal ideas as expressed by the most refined philosophical minds.[1] At the other end of the spectrum, historians such as Robert Darnton use quantitative methods to study the diffusion of books.[2] In this case, the object of investigation is not ideas at all but the distribution of certain material objects. Between these two extreme definitions of intellectual history, the varieties are inexhaustible. There are studies of individual thinkers, of intellectual movements, of disciplines, of collective consciousness, of elite and popular culture. The object of study may be a philosophical treatise, a novel, a painting, a newspaper, a collection of letters, a political document, or something else. The method of investigation may be philological, chronological, psychoanalytic, Marxist, anthropological, or, in extreme cases, historical. If the future of a discipline is guaranteed by its diversity, one can confidently predict many rosy years ahead for intellectual history.

It is possible to argue, however, that the diversity of intellectual history is more an appearance than a reality. Behind the innumerable variations rest a few central themes and assumptions that constitute the basis for a coherent discipline, even though they are not always acknowledged openly. The main works of intellectual history over the past few decades consistently display the following motifs, either explicitly or implicitly: First, there is a Western intellectual tradition that is highly valued and thought to be worthy of study and important for the culture as a whole. Although this tradition contains diverse strains, its unity is predominant. Individuals may disagree about when it began (in ancient Egypt or Greece, Judea or Rome, the Middle Ages or the Renaissance) or about whom or what it includes. But all agree that it must be pursued as an object of study and that it can be disseminated to alert minds in the period of two semesters or three quarters.

Second, the Western intellectual tradition exists in a state of continuous transformation. It is ruled by evolution within continuity. Changes do occur, more or less dramatically, but they only enrich the corpus as a whole, a corpus whose keepers are the intellectual historians themselves. The traits of evolution and continuity assure an enviable epistemological and cultural role for intellectual historians. They embody and recapitulate the entire history. They constitute a vital link between past and present whereby the past becomes identical with the present. Because the tradition is characterized by continuity, the past is domesticated by the historian, shorn of all its strange and threatening difference. A good example of the force of continuity may be seen in the intellectual history of the early modern period. Before the 1960s, important Renaissance systems of belief such as witchcraft, alchemy, and astrology were excluded from the tradition. Since the 1960s, when the Self-Realization Fellowship and the Hare Krishna movement became tolerated if not welcomed by the culture, there has been a new interest in all sorts of previously ignored beliefs of the sixteenth and seventeenth centuries. The Hermetics were discovered and became a component of the great tradition, located in a small but not unrespected corner of the larger whole.[3] Their contestatory potential in relation to Christianity or science was submerged and mitigated, and they joined in the evolutionary parade of great ideas.

Third, the Western intellectual tradition, although it includes some rather bizarre beliefs, promotes a few central values such as reason and freedom. The bearers of these ideas do not remain the same through the centuries or in the annals of intellectual historians, but the values persist and grow nonetheless. If intellectual historians once looked to John Locke and Voltaire for manifestations of the value of freedom, now they may turn to Karl Marx and Sigmund Freud. If David Hume and Immanual Kant once defined the difference between reason and unreason, now George Hegel and Søren Kierkegaard may displace them. In all cases, the victor is the Western tradition.

Fourth, texts are interpreted for consistency and viewed as expressions of ideas within the minds of their creators. Intellectual historians discover in texts the conceptual and moral vision of the writer. The Western intellectual tradition goes beyond the materiality of the printed word to the ideality of spiritual states and expressions. In extreme cases, there can be problems in locating a consistent, noncontradictory intellectual configuration for a given author. Jean-Jacques Rousseau provides an obvious example: Was he a rationalist proponent of Enlightenment values or an asocial romantic retreating from social intercourse into his solitary reveries and paranoid delusions? Did he favor democracy or totalitarianism? How could this proponent of maternal breast-feeding and author of a manual devoted to the most beneficent methods of child rearing dispatch his own children to an orphanage? Was Rousseau an advocate of the advanced form of social organization outlined in the *Social Contract*, did he favor the primitivism of the noble savage, or was his preference for some stage of development between the two? Intellectual historians have argued each of these positions, but very few have resisted the metier's penchant for reconciling differences, collapsing contradictions, and erasing one side of the antimony.

Intellectual history as a discipline is characterized by these four traits: it takes as a given the unity of Western tradition, it sees that tradition's evolution as continuity, it accepts the notion that the tradition's core values are reason and freedom, and it prefers noncontradiction and to assume the ideality of the text. It is legitimate to question the basis of this discipline, to ask if its project is defensible, to investigate its role in the cultural totality, and to propose alternatives to it. In *The Archeology of Knowledge*, Michel Foucault, Professor of the History of Systems of Thought at the Collège de France, sets out on just this task. Not since Wilhelm Dilthey and the debate in Germany over the special epistemological value of *Geisteswissenschaften* as distinguished from *Naturwissenschaften* has intellectual history received a more rigorous and relentless review. Yet Foucault's efforts have been greeted with little enthusiasm by intellectual historians, who have tended instead to regard *The Archeology of Knowledge* as an unwanted intrusion into their domain by a philosopher who is remote from the special considerations of their craft.[4]

In the eyes of some intellectual historians, The Archeology of Knowledge is a reckless and irresponsible rejection of a valuable scientific enterprise. The historians accuse Foucault of producing new categories, such as discourse and archive, that are abstract and inappropriate for use in intellectual history. Those categories, they assert, are incomprehensible, vague, and riddled with contradictions. Far from providing a new basis for intellectual history, Foucault has, in their view, completely abandoned the discipline in favor of a form of structuralism that is incapable of rendering the phenomenon of change intelligible.

Needless to say, I do not agree with this assessment of *The Archeology of Knowledge* or of Foucault's work in general (which often receives similar evaluations). But in order to make a proper judgment of the merits of *The Archeology of Knowledge*, if there are any, it must be placed in the context of Foucault's larger project and that of French poststructuralism in general.

The first task is to determine why Foucault was so dissatisfied with the state of intellectual history that he took the trouble to write a major treatise devoted at least in part to revising it. Could it be that intellectual historians are failing to make progress in the knowledge of the past? Is it possible that their standards are inadequately lofty and their work shoddy? Are the questions they pursue improper or too crudely formulated? Is there, in short, a problem with the methods, theory, or practices within the discipline of intellectual history? Foucault's answer to these questions is simply no. He grants contemptuously that

> to seek in this great accumulation of the already-said the text that resembles "in advance" a later text, to ransack history in order to rediscover the play of anticipations or echoes, to go right back to the first seeds or to go forward to the last traces, to reveal in a work its fidelity to tradition or its irreducible uniqueness, to raise or lower its stock of originality, to say that the Port-Royal grammarians invented nothing, or to discover that Cuvier had more predecessors than one thought, these are harmless enough amusements for historians who refuse to grow up.[5]

Foucault does not take exception to intellectual history because of inadequacy in the quality of its work, at least not in the first instance. Instead, he seeks to revise the nature of intellectual history because of its cultural and ultimately political implications. Like Jacques Derrida, Jacques Lacan, and Gilles Deleuze, Foucault has taken over the theme of decentering humans from their metaphysically privileged position in the Western intellectual tradition. Galileo, Darwin, Marx, and Freud all argued that humankind was not the center of the universe, be it physical, biological, social, or psychological. Each thinker demonstrated that the dominant worldview of the time had given to human beings a special status that was undeserved. That the earth was the center of the universe, that humanity was the apex of creation, a species apart from the rest, that society was a direct reflection of reason and human intention, that the ego was the center of the psyche, the captain of the soul: all these deeply entrenched intellectual positions were overturned by the great detractors of man.

But this conclusion is well known to intellectual historians, the coin of their disciplinary realm. In fact, the theme of the decentering of human kind may be considered part of the Western intellectual tradition. One might think that there is no cause for alarm here. On the contrary, there *is* reason for worry. Foucault and the poststructuralists carry the process of decentering one step further, and by doing so they call into question the foundation of the Western intellectual tradition and its historians as well. The poststructuralists begin their critique where the structuralists left off.[6] The latter had introduced into the intellectual debate the notion that language is not a neutral means for the expression of consciousness. Rather than being a tool at humanity's disposal, language contains its own structure, which shapes consciousness as much or more than consciousness shapes it. From this theme came the notorious structuralist proposition that language was the center of culture, and man its object. Literary critics then began to search in novels not for the intention of the author or for his creative expression, but for the play of language, the internal structure of the text. Anthropologists similarly began to search in so-called primitive societies not for the variety of human expression but for an unconscious pattern of binary oppositions that was analogous to the structuralist view of language.[7] Language and society were thus constituted by a level of intelligibility that was out of phase with human consciousness, behind it and inaccessible to it under normal circumstances.

Poststructuralists rejected the formalist implications of these positions and focused instead on the logic of representation contained within the traditional notion of reason. In his method of deconstruction, for example, Derrida showed how the traditional concept of reason relied on spoken language as a privileged form of communication and implied an identity of reason and reality, an unlimited ability of reason to contain, embody, and represent the real.[8] Using the model of writing, Derrida was able to demonstrate, against the proponents of a logic of identity, that difference pervaded the relation of idea and reality. By the same token, Foucault, in *The Order of Things*, uncovered a level of epistemological ordering in several discourses that constituted the truth beyond the ken of reason.[9] The nature of this episteme was different in different periods of history. Once again reason was dislocated from its immediate continuity with reality. The rational intention of authors had little to do with the constitution of discourses at the level of the episteme.

Our culture, these poststructuralists argue, presumes that reality is available to reason in a direct and immediate fashion, that the Western intellectual tradition continues in a secular form the Judeo-Christian view of God's relation to the world, in which spirit absorbs reality totally and immediately. In the odyssey of reason, from the Greeks to the existentialists, one finds a pervasive myth that reason is continuous with reality, that the former may make itself identical with the latter, and that priests, philosophers, intellectuals, and now scientists are the privileged caretakers of this process. Intellectual historians are the curators of the great museum of reason, redecorating the walls to reflect changing tastes, dusting off long-forgotten productions, in a never-ending effort to preserve and revalidate the precious heritage. By undertaking this task, the discipline of intellectual history, Foucault proclaims, has become an accomplice of logocentrism and must be condemned along with it. Foucault writes in *The Archeology of Knowledge*:

> Continuous history is the indispensable correlative of the founding function of the subject: the guarantee that everything that has eluded him may be restored to him; the certainty that time will disperse nothing without restoring it in a reconstituted unity; the promise that one day the subject—in the form of historical consciousness—will once again be able to appropriate, to bring back under his sway, all those things that are kept at a distance by difference, and find them in what might be called his abode.
>
> (p. 12)

The task of a truly critical science, a new kind of intellectual history that Foucault prefers to call archeology, which he attempts to define in *The Archeology of Knowledge*, will then be "to operate a decentering that leaves no privilege to any center" (p. 205).

It is not Foucault's purpose to destroy history or even intellectual history. He states explicitly: "One must not be deceived: what is being bewailed with such vehemence is not the disappearance of history, but the eclipse of that form of history that was secretly, but entirely, related to the synthetic activity of the subject" (p. 14). His aim instead is to resolve "a crisis that concerns . . . transcendental reflexion." Now that the texts of the past cannot be taken as expressions of the subject because it cannot be assumed that reason is an emanation of consciousness, how can one look at these texts? If one agrees with Foucault and the poststructuralists that cultural assumptions about the major intellectual tendencies and traditions only preserve and perpetuate an unwarranted celebration of the rational subject, then one must take seriously his effort to redefine intellectual history so that it no longer is the witting or unwitting accomplice of logocentrism. "This book," Foucault writes in *The Archeology of Knowledge*, ". . . belongs to that field in which the questions of the human being, consciousness, origin, and the subject emerge, intersect, mingle and separate off" (p. 16).

Foucault places his own discussion of the theory of history in the context of the ongoing project of the Annales school.[10] Beginning with Marc Bloch and Lucien Febvre, later with Fernand Braudel, and more recently with a third generation of Annalistes, this group has labored against the dominant trend of historical writing that relies on a narration of events characterized by intentional acts of individuals or groups. Writing primarily about politics, traditional historians were oblivious, the Annalistes complained, to the underlying, long-term social, economic, and demographic conditions that were the true basis of historical change and continuity. With the writings of Marc Bloch (*Feudal Society*, 1940) and Fernand Braudel (*The Mediterranean*, 1949), the Annales school became notorious for disregarding political events and developing quantitative, serial methods in order to study land tenure systems, price indexes, population curves, climatic shifts, and the like. More recently, Annalistes turned their attention to the domain of intellectual history and produced the concept of *mentalité* to denote collective forms of consciousness and make them available for their analysis.[11]

Foucault regards the work of the Annales school as representative of the current state of the discipline of history. Far from being a disrespectful nihilist berating the historical profession, he sees himself as building on the solid foundation constructed by the Annales. In *The Archeology of Knowledge* his specific task is, given the methods employed by the Annalistes, to elaborate a new theory of history that conceptualizes the objects of their research and clarifies the direction for future study. In the area of intellectual history, the dominant tendency in the work of the Annales school was to reject the assumption of a continuous evolution of reason and substitute for it notions of discontinuity, ruptures, and breaks. "Thus," writes Foucault, "in place of the continuous chronology of reason, which was invariably traced back to some inaccessible origin, there have appeared scales that are sometimes very brief, distinct from one another, irreducible to a single law, scales that bear a type of history peculiar to each one, and which cannot be reduced to the general model of consciousness that acquires, progresses, and remembers" (p. 8). Happily, Foucault finds that the Annalistes have already moved along the line of a Nietzschean critique of traditional intellectual history. They no longer assume the document or text to preserve, however silently, the voice of the subjects, the consciousness of those long dead, the reason of the fathers. Instead, according to Foucault, they acknowledge that documents are simply "monuments," inert traces whose deciphering depends on their being allowed to remain as they are during the act of interpretation, in other words, on the historian's resisting the temptation to attribute to them a human form, a unity and familiarity that bespeaks needs that are within him or her, not the history. Foucault would have history avoid anthropomorphism, the error of re-

ducing the significance of texts to the intentionality of a constitu-
tive subject.

Foucault's goal in *The Archeology of Knowledge* is to reconsti-
tute intellectual history along objectivist lines, whereby the texts
of the Western intellectual tradition would be studied as if they
were large-scale social phenomena. His aim is not to rob texts of
their humanity, to reify them and treat them merely as things,
but to avoid humanizing them falsely. He wants to avoid creating a past in which the historian finds in the world a home for
himself: a cozy, domestic place devoid of the strange and the
alien. He does not want the historian to look to the past for a justification of himself, for a religious sanctification of his own values, because this diminishes history to the level of ideology.

The strategy of dehumanization initiated in *The Archeology of
Knowledge* attempts a drastic reformulation of the field of intellectual history. It is difficult to grasp Foucault's concepts of *monument*, *discourse*, and *archive* just because they are so unfamiliar,
so removed from the normal procedures of the discipline. Yet
when the veils of unfamiliarity are stripped away, however
briefly, one can see that his project does make sense and does offer a new notion of what intellectual history could be about. The
texts of the past can be viewed without resort to the subject and
can reveal a level of intelligibility all their own. The problem of
reading Foucault is not that his writing is abstract, or that his
style is elusive, or that his intent is suspicious at best and mali-
cious at worst. It is rather that he speaks from a place that is new
and strange and perhaps threatening. This is not to say that Foucault's formulation of intellectual history is without difficulties,
but only that it offers a compelling alternative that ought to be
considered.

Foucault prefers to call his new form of intellectual history
"archeology." Archeology works against the grain of intellectual
history, reversing its disciplinary strategies. In Foucault's definition, archeology labors "to untie all those knots that historians
have patiently tied; it increases differences, blurs the lines of

communication, and tries to make it more difficult to pass from one thing to another" (p. 170). Unlike the intellectual historian who moves, as on a continuous path, from the Renaissance to the Reformation, from the Enlightenment to romanticism, then to realism, and so on, the archeologist remains at one site, digging in all directions, unearthing the specificities of a particular discourse. Foucault regards archeology as "the intrinsic description of the monument," or object of historical investigation. He does not elaborate the notion of archeology in much detail, leaving it to denote, at a general level, "a possible line of attack for the analysis of verbal performances" (p. 206).

Such an inadequate level of specification is characteristic of *The Archeology of Knowledge*, and Foucault is quite aware of this limitation. He defends himself by admitting frankly that he took his project only so far and was unable at that point to develop the new form of intellectual history fully and comprehensively. He acknowledges in the conclusion that "this book was written simply in order to overcome certain preliminary difficulties" (p. 210). He warns the reader that he has not yet discovered a satisfactory theory of archeology but only the rough outlines, the beginning stages of such a theory. Given these remarks, one can dismiss the book as premature or accept it as a work in progress that invites contributions from others for further development. There is reason enough based on what is presented in *The Archeology of Knowledge* to select the latter option. If one keeps in mind the caveat that the work is not a finished project, one can review its propositions and evaluate their strengths and weaknesses in an appropriately tentative spirit.

The first theoretical question to be faced by any discipline is the nature of its object. For Foucault, the object of investigation for intellectual history is no longer the ideas of subjects but rather discourse treated as an objective phenomenon. He argues that "discourse is not the majestically unfolding manifestation of a thinking, knowing, speaking subject, but, on the contrary, a totality, in which the dispersion of the subject and his discontinuity with himself may be determined. It is a space of exteriority in which a network of distinct sites is deployed" (p. 55). The object is no longer the minds of individuals expressed in books, which are communicated to others in an endless succession of silent dialogues. The "unities," or points of coherence, of discourse are not those of ideas as traditionally conceived by intellectual historians. Instead, radically new rules must be generated, Foucault thinks, to determine the exact nature of the "unities" of discourse. And this, the new object of intellectual history, is the task of the major portion of *The Archeology of Knowledge*. Now the question is: what kinds of things must historians look for if they intend to study discourses without relying on a transcendental subject?

Once liberated from the subject and all the forms of continuity associated with it (*Geist*, tradition, influence, evolution, book, *oeuvre*), intellectual history can define its object as discourses that are composed of statements that are themselves constituted by rules of formation and have types of relations with other statements. Foucault suggests that, for the purposes of a beginning only, one may regard the empirical disciplines, such as the human sciences, as the field of discourses. In the final analysis, discourses will not be identical with disciplines, but the latter, Foucault believes, are the most sensible place to initiate the labor of discursive analysis. The only reason that is suggested—or, better, implied—for this strategic choice is that these disciplines are characterized, more than any other possible starting point, by unities that are discontinuous, characterized by limits, boundaries, breaks, nonidentities, features that help to reverse the traditional strategy of searching for continuity.

After deciding on the locus of discourses, Foucault puts forth some hypotheses relating to their analysis. With discontinuity and nonidentity as the guiding threads, he turns to the rules of formation and discourse as the basic unity. Discourse is characterized by a set of rules that allow it to act on its object. In order for these rules to constitute a discourse about something, there must exist a set of procedures through which the object may be coherently addressed. The character of such rules is that their nature and effectiveness have nothing to do with spirit, expression, subjects, and so forth. On the contrary, they "define the transformations of . . . different objects, their non-identity through time, the break produced in them, the internal discontinuity that suspends their permanence" (p. 33). In this way Foucault has begun to specify the objects of the analysis of discourse, which, if nothing else, do not rely on the rational subject. He then adds three more features to the analysis: one must look for (1) the relations of connection among statements ("the degree to which they depend on one another, the way in which they interlock or exclude one another" [p. 34]), (2) the stable concepts they depend on, and (3) the themes they pursue.

When intellectual historians go about their business, they begin by picking a topic such as a concept (freedom, for instance), or an individual (Rousseau), or a text (*The Social Contract*). They next look for the connections between instances of their topic (different definitions of freedom in *The Social Contract*) and between their topic and other related topics (the Enlightenment, totalitarian states). Foucault avoids this procedure. He begins with a body of texts that have some externally defined unity (medical treatises in the eighteenth century). He then places in brackets the unities of this body of texts that might have been offered by their authors, the general public, or anyone else. Instead he peruses these texts for recurrent statements, which he then differentiates from other bodies of texts. He searches for clues that will define the discontinuity of this body of texts from others. In this way he believes he can arrive at a form of coherence that defines these texts in themselves. The discourse will then stand out by itself and not be absorbed by any sweeping historical phenomenology of mind.

At this point one may ask with some legitimacy, what possibly could be the purpose of the undertaking that Foucault proposes? For what possible reason would one go to the trouble of poring over masses of obscure, long-forgotten texts and, after great pains, reveal the discourse within them? These texts are not necessarily beautiful or good or true. They are not fine examples of human intellect, likely to arouse awe at the wonders of man's sublime character. Nor are they likely to contain much wisdom that can be passed on to new generations so that humanity's enterprises may be improved, its life elevated, or its motives purified. The texts will permit little enjoyment in the reading; they are not splendid examples of the craft of writing. As likely as not the treatises Foucault would have us attend to will be cramped and cranky, turgid, boring, and uninspired, written by proponents of fanciful projects, by seekers after hopeless delusions, by advocates of ridiculous proposals. Without connecting us to our traditions and with no prospect of improving our future, the archeology of discourses appears to be much like digging the proverbial trench only to be able to fill it up again.

The Archeology of Knowledge, however, does contain an important if only implicit agenda. First, there is the stated task, which must not be minimized, of extricating intellectual history from the morass of logocentrism. Beyond that, however, there also is the implied version of the critique of discourses, of discourses as the locus of a kind of knowledge and power that has become a pervasive form of domination in the twentieth century. *The Archeology of Knowledge* forms a bridge, I would argue, between Foucault's early writings, which attack a process of exclusion wherein power was conceived as a negative force, and his writings of the 1970s, which attack a process of social control wherein power is conceived as a positive force. The journey from one position to the other required the construction of a notion of discourse as practice that eased the passage toward a general critique of advanced industrial society.

In *The Archeology*, Foucault states that he is attempting to determine how social practices can become the object of scientific discourse. He dismisses the effort to reduce discourse to social practice or to some other referent because his strategy is the reverse of that. He states: "Not . . . that such analyses are regarded as illegitimate or impossible; but they are not relevant when we are trying to discover, for example, how criminality could become an object of medical expertise or sexual deviation a possible object of psychiatric discourse" (p. 48). Foucault wants to determine how discourse is a practice that creates objects and, by creating them, determines their nature. In other words, his position is the opposite of Marx's: he does not believe that the mode of production results in the ideology of political economy or liberalism but that the Marxist discourse/practice constitutes an object in which men and women become "economic" agents. This reversal is hard to grasp because it is not simply another form of idealism. On the contrary, Foucault began with the premise that discourses are not the expression of ideas. Between historical materialism, which reduces discourse to social practice, and intellectual history, which reduces social practices to an evolution of ideas, Foucault pursues an intermediate level in which discourse/practices have a form of coherence and a mode of effectivity all their own.

In his inaugural lecture at the Collège de France, "The Discourse on Language," delivered shortly after the appearance of *The Archeology of Knowledge*, Foucault was more explicit about the relation of discourse to power. "I am supposing," he said, "that in every society the production of discourse is at once controlled, selected, organized and redistributed according to a certain number of procedures, whose role is to avert its powers and its dangers, to cope with chance events, to evade its ponderous, awesome materiality."[12] Foucault does not reduce discourse to a material or social referent but constitutes it within the play of power. The "procedures" of discourse are designed to shape and form social activity. Discourse does not act at the behest of power. It is power. Therefore it must be examined on its own terms, dissected scrupulously to uncover its mode of effectivity.

If the concept of discourse serves as a transition to a new concept of power, and if intellectual history is to assume a new role as the critique of this form of power, Foucault fails to confront adequately a number of questions raised by this project. The impression left on the reader by *The Archeology of Knowledge* is that traditional intellectual history is flawed because it does not put into question the Western notion of reason. A new discipline is offered in substitution, one that employs the notion of discourse. The justification for the new discipline is made on positivist grounds: that the new categories fit the data better than the old ones. The data, now discourses, are important to study only because they are there. Foucault writes:

> To describe a group of statements not as the closed, plethoric totality of a meaning, but as an incomplete, fragmented figure; to describe a group of statements not with reference to the interiority of an intention, a thought, or a subject, but in accordance with the dispersion of an exteriority; to describe a group of statements in order to rediscover not the moment or the trace of their origin, but the specific forms of an accumulation, is certainly not to uncover an interpretation, to discover a foundation, or to free constituent acts; nor is it to decide on a rationality, or to embrace a teleology. It is to establish what I am quite willing to call a *positivity*. . . . If, by substituting the analysis of rarity for the search for totalities, the description of relations of exteriority for the theme of the transcendental foundation . . . one is a positivist, then I am quite happy to be one.
>
> (p. 125)

This disarming acceptance of the positivist label satisfies no one and obscures the question of the relation of discourse to power.

Foucault does little better in clarifying the issues related to the question of the history of science. It would appear that his concept of discourse is best suited to writing the history of the sciences, especially the social sciences. Medicine, psychiatry, criminology, political science, and sexology: these have been his dominant concerns, and these discourses seem most appropriately related to the notion of power as positive. In each case, a discourse is generated that is closely associated with practice. In each case, a domain appears in the social context that is defined and shaped by the discourse/practice. But can the same relation be shown to hold in other discourses, such as utopian writings, which make no pretense to scientificity? Foucault speaks to the question at several points in *The Archeology of Knowledge* and "The Discourse on Language" without coming to any convincing conclusion. In one place, he leans toward limiting intellectual history to the sciences, in another he includes the process of a discourse becoming a science, and in still another he takes a broader view of the domain of his discipline.

The question of scope is particularly significant because, in one reading, Foucault's project appears to be that of tracing the rise of certain social science disciplines until they become, in the twentieth century, dominant forms of discourse that constitute a new formation of power. In this reading, discourse becomes the central vehicle of social control, and Foucault provides a means to comprehend and undo it. Archeology aspires to replace Marxism as the new critical theory.

A second reading, equally valid, suggests that discourse is not characterized by an evolutionary rise to dominance but pertains equally to the premodern, modern, and contemporary periods. The seventeenth-century confessional and the twentieth-century psychotherapeutic session are equal examples of the play of discourse. The same would hold for conversations in a fifteenth-century village and in a twentieth-century welfare agency office. In all these instances, discourse plays the same role, has the same weight, reveals the same textuality, and unleashes the same kind of power. According to this reading, however, the archeologist would have to give up any claim to differentiating historical epochs by the form, not just the content, of their discursive practices.

The choice between these two readings of *The Archeology of Knowledge* is undecidable, though, if anything, Foucault's treatment of the question of historical change and his relation to structuralism in the *Archeology* would favor the second reading.

Against the objection that his concept of discourse is ahistorical because it is presented atemporally, Foucault counters flatly that such is not the case. He writes, "I have not denied—far from it—the possibility of changing discourse: I have only deprived the Sovereignty of the subject of the exclusive and instantaneous right to it" (p. 209). According to Foucault, discourses do undergo transformation, but these changes pertain to their internal structure, not to the volition of subjects. To the question of the relation of discursive change to political change, he modestly declines to respond on the ground that his thinking has not yet gone that far.

Another charge often made against Foucault—one that emphasizes the ahistoricity of his categories—is that of structuralism. Like the structuralists, Foucault seems to treat only synchrony, not diachrony. Although no informed reader would claim that Foucault is, like many structuralists, a true formalist, ferreting out the binary oppositions of the object with no concern for referents or *signifiés*, one can establish many parallels between Foucault and structuralist thought. He is obsessed with discontinuity and opposes any reliance on the constituting subject. He is adamantly opposed to organicism, teleology, humanism, and expressivism. Foucault acknowledges that the aims of archeology "are not entirely foreign to what is called structural analysis," but he denies that he is merely transferring a structuralist methodology to a new field (p. 15). His aim instead is to indicate the limits of "the structuralist enterprise" and to restore to history its vitality. "I did not deny history," he proclaims, "but held in suspense the general, empty category of change in order to reveal transformations at different levels" (p. 200).

Structuralist or not, Foucault emerges, in this reading of *The Archeology of Knowledge*, as offering a promising line of development for intellectual history, one that extricates it from an unwanted reliance on logocentric assumptions. He offers a path beyond the long-standing embarrassment of intellectual history: that in its loving exploration of the elaborate mansions of the

Western intellectual tradition it has been unwittingly complicit with that tradition even in its most critical moments. That the *Archeology* does not go far enough in constructing new foundations for the discipline is a fault Foucault openly admits. Yet there are enough hints and indications of the shape of the new field to license further work, both theoretical and empirical.

Most disturbing to me is not the incompleteness of Foucault's categories and project but the fact that I have relied, in this essay, most heavily on the old methods in the pursuit of Foucault's new ones. I have examined the discipline of archeology not as a discourse but as a set of ideas, as the project of an author, as the work of a subject. If I was unable to avoid such retrogression, I can ask if Foucault was the source of the problem. Is it possible to argue without contradiction, as he attempts to do, that discourses are faceless objectivities and, at the same time, attempt consciously to establish such a discourse? Can he create a discipline and yet maintain that disciplines are not created by subjects? For a partial response I turn to Foucault's text: "I am no doubt not the only one who writes in order to have no face. Do not ask who I am and do not ask me to remain the same: leave it to our bureaucrats and our police to see that our papers are in order" (p. 17).

6

History as Knowledge

The previous chapter reproduced an older essay that I first presented at a conference organized by Dominick LaCapra and Steven Kaplan at Cornell University in 1980. The conference was titled "The Future of Intellectual History," and I prepared for it with some misgiving as I had doubts about a positive reply. Social history was then dominant in the profession but more cogently the model of intellectual history as filiation of ideas and their paraphrase had been trenchantly dismantled by Foucault and Derrida. My essay, as you have seen, takes up the challenge of Foucault's critique of intellectual history and offers it to the subdiscipline of intellectual. Other papers at the conference—those of Dominick LaCapra, Martin Jay, Roger Chartier, Hans Kellner, and Keith Baker, to name but a few—introduced similar epistemological moves.[1] This marked a turning point of sorts in the profession: henceforth European intellectual historians took upon themselves the tasks of mediating the linguistic turn for the discipline of history, of introducing historians to the work of poststructuralists and other contemporary continental thinkers such as Jürgen Habermas, and more generally of raising the question of theory and epistemology in the face of a doggedly empiricist scholarly world. Not everyone in the group agreed on all the issues, to be sure, but the general direction of inquiry for the next decades was set. If Hayden White was isolated and virtually excluded from the profession with the publication of *Metahistory* in 1973, the same fate would not befall the next generation. Yet the discipline did not greet the new directions with open arms, and much work remains to be done. It is with that knowledge that I have written this book.

Throughout this work I have been concerned to elucidate the epistemological conditions for cultural history in the context of an emerging postmodern era. Some form of cultural history now dominates the historical profession as new journals, new books, and recent conferences all attest. The question remains, however, as to whether the attention to cultural history is reproducing the problems associated with the shift to social history in the 1970s and 1980s. In other words, are we as cultural historians trapped within the epistemological paradigm of social history? Have we accounted for the mediation of the text both in the documents we study and in the works we write? Have we wrestled with the problem of the changes in the mediations of language, image, and voice in the world around us and introduced problematics derived from that intellectual effort into our investigations into the past? Are the new cultural objects we study and their associated new archives being examined with the same combination of empiricism and realism that characterized the earlier fields of political and social history? Are we still searching for rational agents in positions of victim and rebel? The topic of culture in the age of the mode of information cannot be addressed so directly. In a mediated world, historians need the self-reflexivity afforded by theoretical questioning.[2] This book has been a plea for such change and I propose below a set of curricular innovations that might aid in implementing the change, because questions of practice are always close to the heart in the United States.

History and Theory at University of California, Irvine

A crucial dimension of the development of cultural history is the graduate curriculum of history departments. Unless graduate education in history includes a serious examination of the epistemological protocols of the discipline it is unlikely that significant change in the direction of cultural history is possible. It is not enough to focus attention on certain objects or fields of investigation that one calls "culture," and it is not enough to search in new archives and new bases of documentation that are somehow associated with these objects. The texts of high theory must become an integral part of the course of study, and these must be connected with appropriate works by historians in order to test their fecundity and limitations. The choice of theoretical texts is less important than the question of their role in the development of historical questions. A short discussion of my experience at uc Irvine may clarify the issue.

Since 1973 these theoretical questions have been a central part of the curriculum of graduate study at the history department at uc Irvine. A yearlong course, which I have helped to teach, on the relation of theory to the writing of history has been required of all incoming graduate students. This is not a course in historiography or the philosophy of history but on the theoretical components, issues, and problems in the structuring of historical texts. Each quarter is divided into a five-week segment on reading the works of a theorist and a five-week segment on historians whose work illustrates an appropriation of that theory. Alexis de Tocqueville, Karl Marx, Max Weber, Sigmund Freud, and Michel Foucault have been taught most often, but anthropological theory, feminist theory, neo-Marxist theory, postcolonial theory, and theories of the media and consumer society have also been offered. The purposes of the course are to familiarize the student with current theoretical trends as they apply to history, to advance the self-consciousness of the student as a producer of knowledge, and to further the student's ability to formulate a research question at the level of dissertation writing. The expectations are that the student has not read the theorist before taking the course and has not thought systematically about the theoretical issues in historical texts.

When teaching the course the theoretical themes that I emphasize are

1. the field of research constituted by the theory;
2. the gap between that field and the extant historical materials;
3. the complex relations of two theories in the same research project; and
4. the political implications of the theory.

I shall explain each of these points in turn.

Every theory opens a field of investigation, raising questions to be answered by empirical research. The field may be trivial, but more often it is overly large, intending to encompass all "real" knowledge. In such cases, it is totalizing or reductionist. The work of translating theoretical works into fields of investigation is a proper theoretical task of the historian. In the case of Marx, one may investigate the relation of the means of production to the relations of production in a given time-place, studying how changing technologies or conditions of factory labor affected workers, the relation of workers to capitalists, or that of workers to their families. Or one may examine, still from a Marxist framework, the influence of the economy on politics or ideas. Marx's writings enable questions such as these to be asked, and they indicate why they are important to historical figures and to present-day societies. The significant point is that these are theoretical issues for the historian; they are distinct from but related to empirical concerns.

When a theorist asks a new question that opens a new field, the archives are redefined. The same materials that were used to investigate one question are now redeployed in another research context. A single historical record, then, can yield multiple findings or have several meanings. In the case of portraits of noble families, Philippe Ariès discovered information about concepts of childhood and family relations where before scholars concentrated on artistic styles.[3] In another case, Mary Beth Norton examined probate documents from the colonial and revolutionary period of American history to examine not the economic history of the era, as had been done earlier, but the condition of women.[4] In these instances, the same material artifact yielded multiple types of knowledge. The question asked by the historian, the field of investigation opened by the theory, thus changes the archive, alters the record, and reconfigures the facts. Against the empiricists' belief that historians simply find data or facts in the traces of the past, I argue that the theory one deploys plays a significant role in constituting the evidence. Saying this, however, immediately requires an additional warning that the theory, the field it opens and the questions it makes available for historical research, never quite fit the materials from the past. There is always a gap between the purposes of a historian's investigation and the structure of the texts or information in the archives. This difference is not a sign of the improper intrusion of theory into history, the forcing of facts into some Procrustean bed, but a condition of historical knowledge, an insistent reminder of the separateness of the historian from his or her object, a cue that there cannot be a representation of the past "as it actually was," to cite Ranke's words, because there is always an irreducible breach between the historian's aims, the discipline's state of the study, and production in the past of the records in question.

Often more than one theory inspires a historical project. Put differently, the same research agenda may be approached by more than one framework. Or, again, the same field of investigation may be illuminated by the beacons of more than one theorist. The history of sexuality, for example, may be approached from Freudian, Foucaultian, and feminist perspectives. In these instances, difficulties arise in the use of multiple terminologies, difficulties that have nothing to do with empirical issues of who said what or did what and a what time and place, of the verification of documents, or of the conflict of evidentiary testimony. These represent another sort of theoretical question that requires often difficult clarification in order to avoid serious problems and confusions about the nature of the question being studied.

A final theoretical issue concerns the political domain. Historical study is structured by the present state of the discipline and the present congeries of circumstances known as "the context." Both the discipline and society are saturated by political orientations, large questions of the fate of the species and the planet, questions that pervade, however subtly, every historical work. As Marc Bloch said in *The Historian's Craft,* history is animated not by the love of the past—that is antiquarianism—but by a passion for the present. In the words of this most distinguished historian, "This faculty of understanding the living is, in very truth, the master quality of the historian."[5] It is a proper task of theoretical clarification to explore the political implication of historians' texts not to erase them in the futile endeavor of objectivity but to understand how this aspect enables and restricts the scope of the question.

These four topics constitute the theoretical dimension of historical study, and their exploration is crucial to the vitality of the discipline, to the continuous task of renewing the shape of the field in a manner that is self-reflexive and responsive to new orientations, new ways of figuring knowledge, and new topics of study. It is with these issues in mind that I have turned to the question of cultural history.

Notes

Introduction

1. See Lynn Hunt, ed., *The New Cultural History* (Berkeley: University of California Press, 1989); and Roger Chartier, *Cultural History: Between Practices and Representations*, trans. Lydia Cochrane (London: Polity, 1988).

2. For a good illustration of these debates, see *The American Historical Review* 94, no. 3 (June 1989), in which is reproduced an edited version of an AHA convention panel entitled "The Old History and the New," featuring contributions by Joan Scott, John Toews, Gertrude Himmelfarb, and others. Allan Megill's essay in the same issue, " 'Description,' Explanation, and Narrative in Historiography," points in the gentlest terms to some of the difficulties in the writing of social historians and their predecessors that are now the subjects of dispute with poststructuralists.

3. E. P. Thompson, "History from Below," *Times Literary Supplement* (April 7, 1966), pp. 279–80.

4. E. P. Thompson, "Socialist Humanism: An Epistle to the Philistines," *The New Reasoner*, no. 1 (summer 1957): 122.

5. E. P. Thompson, *The Making of the English Working Class* (New York: Vintage, 1963), p. 9.

6. Peter Novick, *That Noble Dream: The "Objectivity Question" and the American Historical Profession* (New York: Cambridge University Press, 1988) shows that this tendency runs deep in the field of history.

7. Hayden White, *Metahistory: The Historical Imagination in Nineteenth-Century Europe* (Baltimore: Johns Hopkins University Press, 1973). Similar arguments are found, though in language more polemical and opaque, in Sande Cohen, *Historical Culture: On the Recoding of an Academic Discipline* (Berkeley: University of California Press, 1986). See also F. R. Ankersmit, "Historiography and Postmodernism," *History and Theory* 2 (1989): 137–53.

8. Joan Scott, *Gender and the Politics of History* (New York: Columbia University Press, 1989).

9. Robert Berkhofer, *Beyond the Great Story: History as Text and Discourse* (Cambridge: Harvard University Press, 1995), is excellent on this question. See

also the important work by Dominick LaCapra, especially *Soundings in Critical Theory* (Ithaca: Cornell University Press, 1989) and *History, Politics, and the Novel* (Ithaca: Cornell University Press, 1987).

10. Chartier, *Cultural History*, p. 37. I have altered slightly the terms of Chartier's binary oppositions.

11. Robert Darnton, *The Business of Enlightenment: A Publishing History of the Encyclopédie* (Cambridge: Harvard University Press, 1979).

12. Michel de Certeau, *The Practice of Everyday Life*, trans. Steven Rendall (Berkeley: University of California Press, 1984); John Fiske, *Television Culture* (New York: Routledge, 1987); Henry Jenkins, *Textual Poachers* (New York: Routledge, 1992).

13. Chartier, *Cultural History*, p. 44.

14. Carolyn Dean, *The Self and Its Pleasures: Bataille, Lacan, and the History of the Decentered Subject* (Ithaca: Cornell University Press, 1992). Dean indicates how the juridical problem of the insane defendant played a role in the resolution of theoretical issues in Lacan's psychoanalysis.

15. Stephen Greenblatt, "Martial Law in the Land of Cockaigne," in *Shakespearean Negotiations* (Berkeley: University of California Press, 1988), pp. 129–63.

16. See, for example, Marjorie Beale, "The Modernist Enterprise" (unpublished manuscript, mimeographed).

1 Lawrence Stone's Family History

1. Michel Foucault, *The Archeology of Knowledge*, trans. A. M. Sheridan-Smith (New York: Pantheon, 1972), p. 12.

2. See the excellent review by Los Schwoerer, "Seventeenth-Century English Women Engraved in Stone," *Albion* 16, no. 4 (winter 1984): 389–403.

3. *Road to Divorce* presents Stone's historical analysis; *Broken Lives* and *Uncertain Unions* offer in turn case studies on divorce and marriage. All three books were published by Oxford University Press.

4. Peter Laslett, *The World We Have Lost* (New York: Scribner's, 1971), p. 93. See also idem, *Household and Family in Past Time* (Cambridge: Cambridge University Press, 1972) for much of the demographic evidence.

5. Stone, *The Family, Sex and Marriage in England, 1500–1800* (New York: Harper and Row, 1977), p. 658.

6. Gerald Platt and Fred Weinstein, *The Wish to Be Free* (Berkeley: University of California Press, 1969) and *Psychoanalytic Sociology* (Baltimore: Johns Hopkins University Press, 1973). Stone does not directly cite these theorists, but he does rely on Edward Shorter's *The Making of the Modern Family* (New York: Basic, 1975), which does discuss their work, for example, on p. 259.

7. Historians of the family are in deep disagreement over the issue of affectionate relations. Many dispute Stone's contention that only with the emergence of the nuclear family did love become a positive value and characteristic tone within the family. For a different point of view and a review of the historiography on the question, see Carmen Luke, *Pedagogy, Printing and Protestantism: The Discourse on Childhood* (Albany: SUNY Press, 1989). Luke exemplifies the point in contention by warning those who regard premodern parents as cold that "we cannot point the accusatory finger at parents of the past" (p. xi). She thereby assumes that to characterize parents as affectless is a condemnatory gesture, an assumption that is by no means to be granted.

8. For a more recent treatment of these themes, see Barbara Hanawalt, *The Ties That Bound: Peasant Families in Medieval England* (New York: Oxford, 1986). On p. 10 she discusses the emotional qualities of these families with somewhat different conclusions from Stone.

9. Stone's book, of course, is not primarily about the lower classes. This is a marginal topic for him. But I would argue that the *form* of his argumentation in the passage discussed is typical throughout the book, as the next example indicates.

10. Michel Foucault, *Discipline and Punishment: The Birth of the Prison*, trans. Alan Sheridan (New York: Pantheon, 1977).

11. From Charles-Augustin Vandermonde, *Essai sur la manière de perfectionner l'espèce humaine* (Paris: Vincent, 1756), as cited by Bogna Lorence, "Parents and Children in Eighteenth-Century Europe," *History of Childhood Quarterly* 2, no. 1 (summer 1974): 1. For similar evidence, see David Hunt, *Parents and Children in History* (New York: Harper and Row, 1970).

12. Stone, letter to *Harper's*, no. 268 (June 1984): 4–5.

13. Jacques Donzelot, *The Policing of Families*, trans. Robert Hurley (New York: Pantheon, 1979), pp. 220–21. For another approach to family history in relation to the state, see Susan Pedersen, *Family, Dependence, and the Origins of the Welfare State: Britain and France, 1914–1945* (New York: Cambridge University Press, 1993). I thank Douglas Haynes who pointed out this book to me.

14. See Jacques Derrida, "No Apocalypse, Not Now (full speed ahead, seven missiles, seven missives)," *diacritics* 14, no. 2 (summer 1984): 20–31.

15. My allusion is to Derrida's essay "Racism's Last Word," trans. Peggy Kamuf, *Critical Inquiry* 12, no. 1 (autumn 1985): 290–99, which Anne McClintock and Rob Nixon criticized for its ahistoricism in "No Names Apart: The Separation of Word and History in Derrida's 'Le Dernier Mot du Racisme,' " *Critical Inquiry* 13, no. 1 (autumn 1986): 140–53. Derrida's response to the criticism, also translated by Peggy Kamuf, is found on pp. 155–70 of same issue of *Critical Inquiry* as "But beyond . . . (Open Letter to Anne McClintock and Rob Nixon)."

16. See Derek Attridge, Geoff Bennington, and Robert Young, eds., *Poststructuralism and the Question of History* (New York: Cambridge University Press, 1987).

17. Allan Megill, *Prophets of Extremity: Nietzsche, Heidegger, Foucault, Derrida* (Berkeley: University of California Press, 1985), p. 63.

18. The main documents on this controversy are contained in Paul de Man, *Wartime Journalism, 1939–43*, ed. Werner Hamacher, et al. (Lincoln: University of Nebraska Press, 1988); and Werner Hamacher, et al., eds., *Responses: On Paul de Man's Wartime Journalism* (Lincoln: University of Nebraska Press, 1989).

19. See Mark Poster, *The Mode of Information* (Chicago: University of Chicago Press, 1990) and *The Second Media Age* (New York: Blackwell, 1995).

20. See, for example, Theodore Koditschek, "Marxism and the Historiography of Modern Britain: From Engels to Thompson to Deconstruction and Beyond" (unpublished manuscript, mimeographed), p. 21.

21. Gabrielle Spiegel, "History, Historicism, and the Social Logic of the Text in the Middle Ages," *Speculum* 65, no. 1 (January 1990): 60.

22. Lawrence Stone, "History and Post-Modernism," *Past and Present*, no. 131 (May 1991): 217.

23. Lawrence Stone, "Dry Heat, Cool Reason," *Times Literary Supplement*, January 31, 1992, p. 3. See also G. R. Elton, *Return to Essentials* (Cambridge: Cambridge University Press, 1991).

24. Lawrence Stone, "History and Post-Modernism," *Past and Present*, no. 135 (May 1992): 192–93.

2   Textual Agents: History at "the End of History"

1. Stephen Kern, *The Culture of Time and Space: 1880–1918* (Cambridge: Harvard University Press, 1983).

2. Paul Virilio, *The Lost Dimension*, trans. Daniel Moshenberg (New York: Semiotext[e], 1991), p. 31. This is an English translation of *L'espace critique* (Paris: Christian Bourgeois, 1984).

3. Bryan Palmer, *Descent into Discourse: The Reification of Language and the Writing of Social History* (Philadelphia: Temple University Press, 1990), p. iv.

4. For an excellent example of an analysis that indicates the materiality of the text as opposed to reading documents as "the direct, untampered expressions of a unified . . . mind," see Harold Mah, "Suppressing the Text: The Metaphysics of Ethnographic History in Darnton's Great Cat Massacre," *History Workshop* 31 (spring 1991): 1–20.

5. Jacques Derrida, *Of Grammatology*, trans. Gayatri Spivak (Baltimore: Johns Hopkins University Press, 1974), pp. 158–59 and 163. See also David Carroll, *Paraesthetics* (New York: Methuen, 1987), pp. 167–68, which helped me locate some of the Derrida references.

6. Jacques Derrida, *Dissemination*, trans. Barbara Johnson (Chicago: University of Chicago Press, 1981), pp. 35–36.

7. He reminds readers of this in a third use of the term ten years later: "*Text*, as I use the word, is not the book. . . . I . . . recast the concept of text by generalizing it almost without limit, in any case without present or perceptible limit, without any limit that *is*. That's why there is nothing '*beyond* the text' " ("Critical Response," *Critical Inquiry* 13 [autumn 1986]: 167).

8. For antiracist theory, see Stuart Hall, "Minimal Selves," in *Identity: The Real Me* (London: ICA, 1987), p. 45; for feminism, see Joan Scott, "Experience," in Judith Butler and Joan Scott, eds., *Feminists Theorize the Political* (New York: Routledge, 1992), pp. 22–40. Scott has engaged in numerous debates with historians over this issue. For example, see her debate with Bryan Palmer, Christine Stansell, and Anson Rabinbach in *International Labor and Working-Class History* 31 (spring 1987): 1–36; and her debate with Linda Gordon in *Signs* 15, no. 4 (summer 1990): 848–60.

9. See Rob Kling, Spencer Olin, and Mark Poster, eds., *Postsuburban California: The Transformation of Orange County Since World War II* (Los Angeles: University of California Press, 1991).

10. E. P. Thompson, *The Making of the English Working Class* (New York: Vintage, 1963), pp. 12–13. See also the excellent analysis of this most important work by Joan Scott in *Gender and the Politics of History* (New York: Columbia University Press, 1988), chap. 4.

11. Joyce Appleby, Lynn Hunt, and Margaret Jacob, *Telling the Truth About History* (New York: Norton, 1994), pp. 9–10.

12. Peter Novick, *That Noble Dream: The "Objectivity Question" and the American Historical Profession* (New York: Cambridge University Press, 1988), p. 593, notes that the 1986 meetings of the AHA had no such discussions. It should be noted, however, that the convention of 1988 had a panel entitled "The Old History and the New" that included contributions by Theodore Hamerow, Gertrude Himmelfarb, Lawrence Levine, Joan Scott, and John Toews. This was published as a forum in *American Historical Review* 94, no. 3 (June 1989): 654–98. This issue also boasted an essay by Allan Megill and another forum on intellectual history with contributions by David Harlan and David Hollinger.

13. David Hollinger, "Discourse about Discourse about Discourse about Discourse? A Response to Dominick LaCapra," *Intellectual History Newsletter* 13 (1991): 18.

14. E. R. Ankersmit, "Historiography and Postmodernism," *History and Theory* 2 (1989): 152.

15. Novick, *That Noble Dream*, pp. 1–2.

16. On this issue, see the important essay by Hayden White, "The Politics of Historical Interpretation: Discipline and De-Sublimation," *Critical Inquiry* 9 (September 1982): 113–37.

17. "Dialogue with Jacques Derrida," in Richard Kearney, *Dialogues with Contemporary Continental Thinkers* (Manchester: Manchester University Press, 1984), pp. 123–24.

18. Stuart Hall, "Cultural Identity and Diaspora," in Patrick Williams and Laura Chrisman, eds., *Colonial Discourse and Post-Colonial Theory: A Reader* (New York: Harvester Wheatsheaf, 1993), p. 394.

19. Of this very large literature, see especially Homi Bhabha, *Local Cultures* (New York: Routledge, 1993); Rey Chow, *Writing Diaspora* (Bloomington: Indiana University Press, 1993); Ernesto Laclau, ed., *The Making of Political Identities* (New York: Verso, 1994); and "The Question of Identity," *October* 61 (special issue) (summer 1992).

20. See, for example, Edward Berenson, *The Trial of Madame Cailliaux* (Berkeley: University of California Press, 1992), p. 8; and Natalie Davis, "Stories and the Hunger to Know," *Yale Journal of Criticism* 5, no. 2 (1992): 161, where she calls for "microhistories" of the discipline of history.

21. Thomas Haskell, "Objectivity Is Not Neutrality: Rhetoric vs. Practice in Peter Novick's *That Noble Dream*," *History and Theory* 29 (1990): 141.

22. Sande Cohen, *Historical Culture: On the Recoding of an Academic Discipline* (Berkeley: University of California Press, 1986); and Elizabeth Ermarth, *Sequel to History: Postmodernism and the Crisis of Representational Time* (Princeton: Princeton University Press, 1992).

23. Jacques Derrida, *The Other Heading: Reflections on Today's Europe*, trans. Pascale-Anne Brault and Michael Naas (Bloomington: Indiana University Press, 1992); idem, "Back from Moscow in the U.S.S.R.," in Mark Poster, ed., *Politics, Theory, and Contemporary Culture* (New York: Columbia University Press, 1993), pp. 197–235.

24. Idem, *Specters of Marx: The State of the Debt, the Work of Mourning, and the New International*, trans. Peggy Kamuf (New York: Routledge, 1994), p. 170.

25. See Perry Anderson's "The Ends of History," an informative intellectual history of the concept of the end of history, including discussions of Hegel, Kojève, and Fukuyama, in *A Zone of Engagement* (New York: Verso, 1992), pp. 279–375.

26. See Mark Poster, *Existential Marxism in Postwar France* (Princeton: Princeton University Press 1975), for a review and analysis of these discussions.

27. For an example of such an objection by a Marxist, see Aijaz Ahmad, "Reconciling Derrida: 'Specters of Marx' and Deconstructive Politics," *New Left Review* 208 (November/December 1994): 88–106. Ahmad does not confront Derrida's critique of the logocentrism in Marx, but he does raise important questions about the ability of deconstruction to critique its own history and avoid a rhetoric of innocence. For a more favorable and probing reading of Derrida's book by a Marxist theorist, see Fredric Jameson,

"Marx's Purloined Letter," *New Left Review* 209 (January/February 1995): 75–109.

28. Anderson disagrees sharply with this judgment ("The Ends of History," p. 333).

29. Francis Fukuyama, *The End of History and the Last Man* (New York: Avon, 1992), p. 211. The original essay appeared as "The End of History?" *The National Interest* 18 (winter 1989): 3–18.

30. See, for example, Wendy Brown, *Manhood and Politics: A Feminist Reading of Political Theory* (Totowa, N.J.: Rowman and Littlefield, 1988), pp. 180–83, for an analysis of the masculine view of politics in relation to tests of will in defiance of life.

31. Anderson puts the issue this way: "The emancipation of women has achieved more gains in the West over the past twenty years than any other social movement. . . . At the same time, it remains massively far away from real sexual equality, whose ultimate conditions are still scarcely imaginable today" ("The Ends of History," pp. 356–57). The question is, to what extent is "scarcely imaginable" a function of masculine bias?

32. Jean-François Lyotard, *The Postmodern Condition*, trans. Geoff Bennington and Brian Massumi (Minneapolis: University of Minnesota Press, 1984).

33. Fredric Jameson, *Postmodernism; or, The Cultural Logic of Late Capitalism* (Durham, N.C.: Duke University Press, 1991).

34. Gianni Vattimo, *The End of Modernity*, trans. Jon Snyder (Baltimore: Johns Hopkins University Press, 1991), p. 4.

35. For a critical discussion of this discourse, see Lutz Niethammer, *Posthistoire: Has History Come to an End?*, trans. Patrick Camiller (New York: Verso, 1992). For a comparison of the postmodern to posthistoire, see Allan Stoekl, "'Round Dusk: Kojève at 'The End,' " *Postmodern Culture* 5, no. 1 (September 1994) (electronic journal).

36. For an analysis of the paradox of the position of the observer, albeit without the constructivist or historicist framework of postmodernity, see Niklaus Luhmann, "The Paradoxy of Observing Systems," *Cultural Critique* 31 (fall 1995): 37–56.

37. For a different characterization of this conundrum, see Jean Baudrillard, *The Illusion of the End*, trans. Chris Turner (Stanford, Calif.: Stanford University Press, 1994).

38. Paul Virilio, "The Last Vehicle," in D. Kamper and C. Wulf, eds., *Looking Back on the End of the World*, trans. David Antal (New York: Semiotext[e], 1989), p. 118. Also see idem, *The End of Modernity*, p. 6.

39. Reinhart Koselleck, *Futures Past: On the Semantics of Historical Time*, trans. Keith Tribe (Cambridge: MIT Press, 1985), p. 275.

40. Kathleen Burnett, "The Scholar's Rhizome: Networked Communication Issues" (kburnett@gandalf.rutgers.edu) explores this issue with convincing logic.

41. For a discussion of the use of hypertext in the humanities, see George Landow, *Hypertext: The Convergence of Contemporary Critical Theory and Technology* (Baltimore: Johns Hopkins University Press, 1992).

42. For critique of Derrida's politics of the ghost, see Sue Golding, "Virtual Derrida," in Jelica Sumic-Riha, ed. *Philosophic Fictions* (Slovenia: Academy of Philosophy, 1994–95).

43. See Appleby, Hunt, and Jacob, *Telling the Truth*, p. 271, where "new thinking" includes "a return to the intellectual center of the Western experience since the seventeenth century."

3   Furet and the Deconstruction of 1789

1. Marc Bloch, *The Historian's Craft*, trans. Peter Putnam (New York: Vintage, 1964); Carl Becker, *Everyman His Own Historian* (New York: Crofts, 1935); Pieter Geyl, *Napoleon: For and Against*, trans. Olive Renier (New Haven: Yale University Press, 1949); G. P. Gooch, *History and Historians in the Nineteenth Century* (Boston: Beacon, 1959); Edward Hallet Carr, *What Is History?*, 2d ed. (New York: Knopf, 1962); Arnold Toynbee, *A Study of History*, 2d ed. (New York: Oxford University Press, 1947).

2. See Steven Kaplan, *Adieu 89*, trans. André Charpentier and Rémy Lambrechts (Paris: Fayard, 1993), pp. 78–82, for a treatment of *Interpreting the French Revolution* as a political text.

3. Jean-Pierre Hirsch, "Pensons la Révolution française," *Annales: E. S. C.* 35 (1980): 331.

4. François Furet, *Interpreting the French Revolution*, trans. Elborg Forster (New York: Cambridge University Press, 1981), p. 3.

5. Idem, *In the Workshop of History*, trans. Jonathan Mandelbaum (Chicago: University of Chicago Press, 1984), p. 20.

6. Furet repeats this warning and this argument in a slightly different form on p. 117: "But lest we should fall prey to complete relativism, which would consist of judging different readings of the past by how they fit into the present, we must try to understand the different intellectual mediations by which an historian's experiences and assumptions make their way into his work."

7. Elaine Showalter, *The Female Malady: Women, Madness, and English Culture, 1830–1980* (New York: Penguin, 1985), p. 61 and passim. Showalter is a literary critic by training, not a historian. Yet her book is a history of women's insanity in the nineteenth century, and it illustrates extremely well the historian's practice of finding resistance among the oppressed in direct statements by them. I am told that Showalter has second thoughts about the success of

her book precisely because she recognizes as problematic this figure of agency.

8. Jacques Rancière, *Les mots de l'histoire: Essai de poétique du savoir* (Paris: Seuil, 1992), pp. 79–88, brilliantly illuminates Furet's critique of the point of view of the historical subject.

9. Lynn Hunt, review of *Interpreting the French Revolution, History and Theory* 20 (1981): 313.

10. Ernesto Laclau and Chantal Mouffe, *Hegemony and Socialist Strategy* (London: Verso, 1985).

11. See Mona Ozouf, *La fête révolutionnaire, 1789–1799* (Paris: Gallimard, 1976).

12. Ernesto Laclau, *New Reflections on the Revolution of Our Time* (New York: Verso, 1990), p. 21.

13. Jürgen Habermas, *The Structural Transformation of the Public Sphere: An Inquiry into a Category of Bourgeois Society*, trans. Thomas Burger (Cambridge: MIT Press, 1989).

14. See Joan Landes, *Women and the Public Sphere in the Age of the French Revolution* (Ithaca: Cornell University Press, 1988).

15. Roger Chartier, *The Cultural Origins of the French Revolution*, trans. Lydia Cochrane (Durham: Duke University Press, 1991), p. 165.

16. Keith Baker, *Inventing the French Revolution: Essays on French Political Culture in the Eighteenth Century* (New York: Cambridge University Press, 1990), pp. 4–5.

17. Lynn Hunt, *Politics, Culture, and Class in the French Revolution* (Berkeley: University of California Press, 1984), pp. 221, 178.

18. Ann Rigney, *The Rhetoric of Historical Representation: Three Narrative Histories of the French Revolution* (New York: Cambridge University Press, 1991), p. xi.

19. On this theme, see also Joan Landes, "Representing the Body Politic: The Paradox of Gender in the Graphic Politics of the French Revolution," in Sara Melzer and Leslie Rabine, eds., *Rebel Daughters: Women and the French Revolution* (New York: Oxford University Press, 1992), pp. 15–37.

20. Robert Darnton, "Revolution Sans Revolutionaries," *New York Review of Books*, January 31, 1985, pp. 21–22.

21. Philippe Carrard, *Poetics of the New History: French Historical Discourse from Braudel to Chartier* (Baltimore: Johns Hopkins University Press, 1992), p. 198.

4   Michel de Certeau and the History of Consumerism

1. Mark Poster, ed., *Baudrillard: Selected Writings*, trans. Jacques Mourrain (Stanford: Stanford University Press, 1989).

2. See, for example, "Two Lectures" and "Truth and Power," in Colin Gor-

don, ed., *Power/Knowledge: Selected Interviews and Other Writings, 1972–1977* (New York: Pantheon, 1980).

3. See "What Is Enlightenment?" in Paul Rabinow, ed., *The Foucault Reader* (New York: Pantheon, 1984), pp. 32–50. Also of interest on the question of resistance is Lawrence Kritzman, ed., *Michel Foucault: Politics, Philosophy, Culture, Interviews and Other Writings, 1977–1984* (New York: Routledge, 1988).

4. See Roland Barthes, "The Discourse of History," p. 139, and "The Reality Effect," in *The Rustle of Language*, trans. Richard Howard (New York: Hill and Wang, 1986).

5. Michel de Certeau, *The Writing of History*, trans. Tom Conley (New York: Columbia University Press, 1988), p. 44.

6. Idem, *Heterologies: Discourse on the Other*, trans. Brian Massumi (Minneapolis: University of Minnesota Press, 1986), p. 203.

7. Michel Foucault, *Discipline and Punish: The Birth of the Prison*, trans. Alan Sheridan (New York: Pantheon, 1977), p. 31.

8. Michel de Certeau, *The Practice of Everyday Life*, trans. Steven Rendall (Berkeley: University of California Press, 1984), p. xi.

9. Andreas Huyssen, "Mass Culture as Woman: Modernism's Other," in Tania Modleski, ed., *Studies in Entertainment: Critical Approaches to Mass Culture* (Bloomington: Indiana University Press, 1986), pp. 188–208.

10. E. P. Thompson, *The Making of the English Working Class* (New York: Vintage, 1963).

11. Neil McKendrick, John Brewer, and J. H. Plumb, *The Birth of Consumer Society: The Commercialization of Eighteenth-Century England* (Bloomington: Indiana University Press, 1982).

12. Judith Schneid Lewis, in *Journal of Social History* 18 (winter 1984): 313.

13. John R. Gillis, in *Journal of Interdisciplinary History* 14 (spring 1984): 870. Even the anthropologist Grant McCracken, in *Culture and Consumption: New Approaches to the Symbolic Character of Consumer Goods and Activities* (Bloomington: Indiana University Press, 1988), recognizes McKendrick has the pioneer of the history of consumption, applauding his book as "the most thorough, well-grounded and impressive of the works" in this field (p. 4). McCracken even claims that the work is beyond criticism: "McKendrick's contribution to this question is so important and remarkable that criticism has a churlish quality" (pp. 5–6). His major complaint with the work is that McKendrick missed the origin of consumer society, which was in the Elizabethan period (p. 28).

14. Rosalind Williams, in *Technology and Culture* 25 (April 1984): 339.

15. See B. A. Holderness's review in *English Historical Review* 99 (January 1984): 122–24. Other critical reviews are Pat Rogers, "The Power of Fashion," *Times Literary Supplement*, June 15, 1984, p. 668; and Janet Oppenheim, in *American Historical Review* 88 (October 1983): 977–78.

16. Colin Campbell, a sociologist, in *The Romantic Ethic and the Spirit of Modern Consumerism* (New York: Blackwell, 1987), also criticizes McKendrick for theoretical ineptness (p. 19). He puts more emphasis than I on the role of Veblenesque emulation in McKendrick's account of the origin of consumer society but also concludes that the latter's "explanation" of the birth is inadequate. Campbell points to the need to look at cultural factors but fails to question whether the eighteenth century is the proper locus in the first place.

5   The Future According to Foucault: *The Archeology of Knowledge* and Intellectual History

1. Some of Lovejoy's methodological statements may be found in *The Great Chain of Being* (Cambridge: Harvard University Press, 1936), chap. 1, and in "Reflections on the History of Ideas," *Journal of the History of Ideas* 1 (January 1940): 3–23.

2. A good example of this method is Robert Darnton, *The Business of Enlightenment: A Publishing History of the Encyclopédie* (Cambridge: Harvard University Press, 1979).

3. Frances Yates, *Giordano Bruno and the Hermetic Tradition* (Chicago: University of Chicago Press, 1964).

4. Allan Megill, "Foucault, Structuralism, and the Ends of History," *Journal of Modern History* 51 (1979): 451–503.

5. Michel Foucault, *The Archeology of Knowledge*, trans. A. M. Sheridan Smith (New York: Pantheon, 1972), p. 144.

6. Fredric Jameson, *The Prison-House of Language* (Princeton: Princeton University Press, 1972). For the earlier background, see Mark Poster, *Existential Marxism in Postwar France* (Princeton: Princeton University Press, 1975).

7. Claude Lévi-Strauss is the best representative of structuralism in anthropology. A good introduction is *Structural Anthropology*, 2 vols. (New York: Doubleday, Anchor, 1963, 1976).

8. Jacques Derrida, *Of Grammatology*, trans. Gayatri C. Spivak (Baltimore: Johns Hopkins University Press, 1976).

9. Michel Foucault, *The Order of Things* (New York: Pantheon, 1970).

10. For an examination of this relationship, see Robert D'Amico, "Four Books on or by M. Foucault," *Telos* 36 (spring 1978): 169–83.

11. The notion of *mentalité* remains poorly defined. For examples of recent work of the Annales school, see *Faire de l'histoire*, ed. Jacques Le Goff (Paris: Gallimard, 1974), and on the Annales school, see Traian Stoianovich, *French Historical Method: The* Annales *Paradigm* (Ithaca, N.Y.: Cornell University Press, 1976).

12. The address is reproduced in Foucault, *Archeology*, where this quotation appears on p. 216.

6   In Place of a Conclusion: History as Knowledge

1. The proceedings were published as Dominick LaCapra and Steven Kaplan, eds., *Modern European Intellectual History: Reappraisals and New Perspectives* (Ithaca, N.Y.: Cornell University Press, 1982).

2. For an excellent discussion of this issue, see Robert Berkhofer, *Beyond the Great Story: History as Text and Discourse* (Cambridge: Harvard University Press, 1995).

3. Philippe Ariès, *Centuries of Childhood: A Social History of Family Life*, trans. Robert Baldick (New York: Knopf, 1962).

4. Mary Beth Norton, *Liberty's Daughters: The Revolutionary Experience of American Women, 1750–1800* (Boston: Little Brown, 1980).

5. Marc Bloch, *The Historian's Craft*, trans. Peter Putnam (New York: Vintage, 1964), p. 43.

Index